SIGNS IN CULTURE

Signs in

**ROLAND
BARTHES
TODAY**

in

Culture

**Edited by Steven Ungar
and Betty R. McGraw**

UNIVERSITY OF IOWA PRESS ꙮ IOWA CITY

University of Iowa Press, Iowa City 52242
Printed in the United States of America
First edition, 1989

Design by Martha Farlow

"Remembering Roland Barthes" is reprinted from the *Nation* (November 20,
1982); "In Memoriam Roland Barthes," with "The Contract: A Stele for Roland
Barthes," is reprinted from *Cream City Review* 6 (1980). "The Two Barthes" is
reprinted from *La Troisième République de Lettres, de Flaubert à Proust* (Paris:
Editions du Seuil, 1983). "The Discourse of Desire" is reprinted from *MLN* 103
(1988).

Library of Congress Cataloging-in-Publication Data

Signs in culture: Roland Barthes today/edited by Steven Ungar and
Betty R. McGraw.
    p. cm.
  Includes index.
  ISBN 0-87745-245-8
  1. Barthes, Roland. 2. Semiotics. I. Ungar, Steven.
II. McGraw, Betty R.
P85.B33S54 1990   89-32171
302.2—dc20   CIP

In memory of Egon Ungar (1914–1986)
and for Gene, and friendship

*Pour entrer en nous, un être a été obligé
de se plier au cadre du temps; ne nous
apparaissant que par minutes succes-
sives, il n'a jamais pu nous livrer de lui
qu'un seul aspect à la fois, nous débiter
de lui qu'une seule photographie.*
   —*Marcel Proust,* A la recherche
     du temps perdu *(III, 478)*

*In order to enter into us, another per-
son must first have assumed the form,
have adapted himself to the framework
of time; appearing to us only in a succession of momentary flashes, he has
never been able to reveal to us more than
a single photograph of himself.*
   —*Marcel Proust,* Remembrance of
     Things Past *(III, 487)*

Contents

STEVEN
UNGAR AND
BETTY R.
MCGRAW

Introduction

_____

Starting with Saussure

What is semiology and what have Roland Barthes's writings contributed to the study of signs? A number of preliminary remarks are in order. At first glance, these two questions seem concise and straightforward. A closer reading, however, reveals a degree of complexity in that the definition called for by the first elides a significant temporal or historical concern. The elision is well illustrated by reformulating the question as that of what semiology is _today_. Understood in this way, answering the first question requires not just a definition but a reassessment that might distinguish present from past conceptions. Semiology exists today, but its current forms and practices differ significantly from those of ten, twenty, and thirty years ago. What are those differences and how might they be illustrated in terms of Barthes's evolved practice of semiology?

The question of Barthes's contribution to the study of signs can be raised via vocabulary and tradition. To begin, his approach derives more from semiology than from semiotics—that is, more from the study of the life of signs within society set forth in Ferdinand de Saussure's 1916 *Course in General Linguistics* than from considerations of the sign and its interpretation in the writings of Charles Saunders Peirce and Charles Morris. The latter tradition is older, with ties to classical antiquity and to questions of language and meaning such as those raised in Plato's Socratic dialogue "Cratylus." Over the past thirty years, the popularity of structural analysis and its avatars among students of literature and the arts has favored the Saussurean variant and extended it toward a number of applications. The evolved practice of semiotics after Peirce and Morris most often consists of rigorous inquiry into meaning on the part of logicians, linguists, and the occasional behaviorist concerned with an empirical study of communication. Where semiotics has seemingly been relegated to the academic department or the laboratory, semiology has increasingly engaged a variety of cultural phenomena ranging from fictional and nonfictional narratives to photography, advertising, clothing, and food. This extension has, in turn, led to departures from both Peirce's logical ("quasi-necessary") study of the sign's features and the Saussurean project of a general science: "Semiology would show what constitutes signs, what laws govern them. Since the science does not yet exist, no one can say what it would be; but it has a right to existence, a place staked out in advance. Linguistics is only a part of the general science of semiology; the laws discovered by semiology will be applicable to linguistics, and the latter will circumscribe a well-defined area within the mass of anthropological facts."[1]

The eight essays in the present collection engage these concerns in a reassessment of Roland Barthes's writings on the life of signs. But where the *Course* proposes "*the life of signs within society*" as the object of a future semiology, we redirect our reassessment instead toward the material practices, forms, and institutions of signs in culture. The choice of culture instead of society is meant to be taken as inclusive rather than dismissive. It is motivated by considerations that devolve from the *Course*'s well-known organization around two sets of binary oppositions: the first pertaining to language and speech (*langue* and *parole*), and the second to acoustic image and concept (*signifiant* and *signifié*, also known in English as "signifier" and "signified").[2] In addition to these formal oppositions, the Saussurean model is founded on a premise of the linguistic sign's arbitrary nature that bears directly on the evolution of Barthes's own semiology. What is referred to in the *Course* as the arbitrary connection between signifier and signified is often misconstrued as unmotivated.

Thus, following an example given in the *Course*, there is no natural or inner connection between the signified "ox" and its signifier *b-ö-f* on one side of the border and *o-k-s* (*Ochs*) on the other (Saussure, p. 68). In fact, the point of the passage is to reject any natural link in favor of a relationship that occurs by convention and that allows for a certain degree of slippage between various differences in pronunciation and accent to associations of meaning that can be personal and collective. The relationships between signifiers and signifieds within a particular language are indeed arbitrary. But once established, that very system or configuration of signs exists as a distinctive entity that can be studied within the specific temporal and spatial elements of its occurrence. Jonathan Culler marks the point well: "Neither the signifier nor the signified contains an essential core which time cannot touch. Because it is arbitrary, the sign is totally subject to history, and the combination at a particular moment of a given signifier and signified is a contingent result of the historical process."[3] The sign is itself historical over and above any sense of arbitrariness that enters into its production. Consequently, it can always be studied as an utterance or instance of speech within language at the convergence of synchronic and diachronic axes.

Barthes and other readers of Saussure's *Course* have also contended with a related point whose complexity makes for a seeming paradox: while the linguistic sign is taken to be a historical phenomenon, it is best understood by a synchronic analysis that extracts it from the ongoing processes of semiosis within which it occurs. As a result, many readers see the semiology outlined in the *Course* as the model of an ahistorical analysis when the priority of synchronic analysis does not exclude a diachronic study of the sign across time. The point is made in a passage that begins as follows: "Synchronic truth seems to be the denial of diachronic truth, and one who has a superficial view of things imagines that a choice must be made; this is really unnecessary; one truth does not exclude the other" (Saussure, p. 96). The conclusion of the same chapter formulates clear definitions of what are referred to as the two parts of linguistics:

> *Synchronic linguistics* will be concerned with the logi-
> cal and psychological relations that bind together coexist-
> ing terms and form a system in the collective mind of
> speakers.
>
> *Diachronic linguistics,* on the contrary, will study re-
> lations that bind together successive terms not perceived
> by the collective mind but substituted for each other with-
> out forming a system. (Saussure, pp. 99–100)

The emphasis on systematic concerns in the *Course* illustrates the extent to which the analysis of language as a unit of
study is considered an alternative to historical and static view-
points. Saussure's future semiology is set apart from the domi-
nant practice of the period, a philology that studied different languages at a single historical moment or a single language over
time. The scientific project of approaching language as a discrete
unit of study does not keep Saussure (or his editors, to be more
precise) from noting self-consciously that the unit in question is
superficial in theory, whereas the diversity of idioms hides a profound unity. If Saussure occasionally hovers between diversity
and unity, he ultimately opts for the latter. The passage quoted
above concludes with the following caveat: "Whichever way we
look in studying a language, we must put each fact in its own
class and not confuse the two methods" (Saussure, p. 99). From
this, we consider at least two provisional consequences. First, the
Saussurean emphasis on the study of language as a sign system
contains an implicit diachronic element that is recognized but
never fully explored. Fredric Jameson rightly notes the plain fact
that one cannot have it both ways: "Once you have begun by separating diachronic from synchronic, in other words, you can never
really put them back together again."[4] Readers of the *Course* who
collapse the distinction between the synchronic and diachronic
models mistake a critical self-consciousness for a deeper ambivalence that the Saussurean model simply does not play out.

A second consequence of the synchronic-diachronic distinction set forth in the *Course* is of longer term and directly related
to Barthes's evolved practice of semiology. It concerns a change
in emphasis to speech and the signifier (*parole* and *signifiant*, respectively) that compensates—some might say excessively—for
the Saussurean emphasis on language as system. In part, the

change is historically determined. It occurs as part of the structuralist revision of the Saussurean model visible in the writings of Lévi-Strauss, Lacan, and—notably—Barthes. This change is also associated with the mid-1960s writings of Michel Foucault and Jacques Derrida that herald the varied practices of what is known as poststructuralism. For many readers, *S/Z* (1970) is the text in which Barthes most notably departs from the canonical model of semiology set forth in the *Course* toward a practice of interpretation that Barthes openly identifies as plural, openended, and nothing less than explosive. Yet there is reason to locate a significant departure from the Saussurean model as early as the essays that were republished in 1957 under the title of *Mythologies*. Writing in 1972, Jameson sees Barthes's role in the structuralist projection as essentially that of sociologist (Jameson, p. 146). Another reader sees Barthes's semiology as a vehicle for conveying personal interpretive insights. As such it opposes both Peirce's philosophical inquiry into the logic of meaning and the empirical science outlined in Saussure's *Course*.[5]

Mythologies ranks alongside Lévi-Strauss's *Structural Anthropology* (1958) as a major extension that also revises the Saussurean model in what has been called the heroic period of structural analysis in Paris between 1955 and 1970. In retrospect, the liberatory and revolutionary ambitions of that period were not always borne out by change at the levels of institution and discipline. At the same time, however, it is clear that the revised model of semiology appropriated in the name of structural analysis has been widely influential in changing practices of literary theory and criticism on an international scale, even when—especially when—that influence has been an object of debate and polemic. Ironically, any assessment of Barthes's contribution to the study of signs must focus in part on the author of "The Death of the Author" (1968) in what is less an interpretation of the work in terms of the author's life than an attempt to follow through what the closure of that work in the wake of the author's actual death left behind as an uncompleted project.

Barthes's Three Semiologies

Barthes's 1976 election to the Collège de France as first chair of literary semiology marked a curious rite of passage. For a writer-critic whose perspective on the French university system had always been external, it was nothing less than a vindication that legitimated the study of signs he had begun in his writing some twenty years earlier in *Mythologies*. Barthes's semiology of the 1950s had approached myth as a language system in which meaning was produced by a willful confusion of nature and history. Myth was a product of the interplay between direct and indirect meanings: a two-part invention or double-tiered system of denotation and connotation whose structure he sought to systematize. *Mythologies* was an exemplary study of how meaning and value occur in everyday life. Its short analyses on the popular press, advertising, photographs, and films were perceptive and often amusing. Taken as a whole, they showed how the social coherence of France in the mid-1950s—associated in large part with lower-middle-class Paris—was a composite of variable factors ranging from economic class and profession to regional identity, religion, and a visceral chauvinism staged as a patriotic attachment to flank steak and French fries (*bifteck-frites*).

The descriptive element in *Mythologies* emphasized the interplay among these variables as open and reversible to a point where the equation of culture with spectacle became more or less total. But the confusion of nature and history detected in *Mythologies* was anything but innocent. The signs of everyday life were also the marks of ideology and cultural formation which Barthes sought to expose and to denounce: "I wanted to track down, in the decorative display of *what-goes-without-saying*, the ideological abuse which, in my view, is hidden there."[6] The 1970 preface to a new edition of *Mythologies* announced a meaningful shift. Barthes still posited the norm of bourgeois as "the enemy" to be denounced, but assigned to that denunciation a more radical objective: "No denunciation without an appropriate method of detailed analysis, no semiology which cannot, in the last analysis, be acknowledged as *semioclasm*" (*Mythologies*, p. 9). This second conception of semiology recognized the network of rules, constraints, oppressions, and repressions that govern the exchange of signs in society and that are miniaturized in the grammar and rhetoric of the sentence. It also recognized how the previous claims made for semiology as a science of signs invariably opposed the critical function that Barthes now wanted to assign to it.

The revised practice of semiology as semioclasm contested the claims of a scientific semiology. But its liberatory ambitions ultimately extended the very practices and institutions of authority it sought to change: "Political bodies were seized with a kind of moral excitement, and even when claims were being made for pleasure, the tone was threatening. Thus we have seen most proposed liberations, those of society, those of culture, of art, of sexuality, articulated in the forms of the discourse of power. We took credit for restoring what had been crushed, without seeing what else we crushed in the process" ("Inaugural Lecture," p. 472). Semioclasm was symptomatic of the contradictions that beset those post-1968 reforms of literature, criticism, and philosophy in France that held revolutionary ambitions. Its failure was in large part a measure of those ambitions. It resulted from a dependence on conceptions of authority and culture whose radicality made them nearly inoperable.

At the same time, Barthes's initial revision of semiology did not adequately account for the ability of advanced capitalist societies to institutionalize, diffuse, and absorb liberatory contestation. The attempt to break the signs of a culture and a society perceived as oppressive only led to new signs and new oppression. If semiology could not break out of or away from semiosis and from institutions of cultural power, what realistic alternative to the scientific conception of semiology was possible? By 1977, Barthes was addressing this question from within a cultural institution of national authority and in the immediate context of a ritual passage organized around apophasis, the trope of simultaneous assertion and denial. How could the self-proclaimed marginal figure use his newly attained authority once he was no longer marginal?

Election to the Collège de France provided Barthes with another opportunity to recast his practice and, as he puts it, continue the Greek paradigm. Barthes's final conception of semiology evolved from a denunciation of language worked on by ideology through a more politicized notion equating language with discourse. After semiology and semioclasm, then, came *semiotropy*: "Turned toward the sign, this semiology is captivated by and receives the sign, treats and, if need be, imitates it as an imaginary spectacle."[7] Barthes invokes the dubious status of his revised semiology at the very moment when it is legitimized within a cultural institution.

In such terms, semiotropy can be seen as both a *negative* and a *positive* semiology. It is negative in that its ancillary relation to a science of signs precludes any claims to associate it with a meta-language or explanatory system distinct from its critical object: "I cannot function *outside* language, treating it as a target, and *within* language, treating it as a weapon" ("Inaugural Lecture," p. 473). Second, while semiotropy can provide an operational protocol to facilitate certain sciences, it should not be misconstrued as a discrete discipline to be used on its own for the problem-solving that is integral to scientific practice: "In other words, semiology is not a grid; it does not permit a direct apprehension of the real through the imposition of a general transparency which would render it intelligible. It seeks instead to elicit the real, in places and by moments, and it says that these efforts to elicit the real are possible without a grid. It is in fact precisely when semiology comes to be a grid that it elicits nothing at all. We can therefore say that semiology has no substitutive role with regard to any discipline" ("Inaugural Lecture," p. 474).

Those who remained committed to a conception of structural analysis that semiotropy no longer upheld saw the evolved position in the inaugural lecture as a betrayal or a reversal when, in fact, Barthes had stated misgivings over semiology from the start, in *Mythologies:* "I cannot countenance the traditional belief which postulates a natural dichotomy between the objectivity of the scientist and the subjectivity of the writer, as if the former were endowed with a 'freedom' and the latter with a 'vocation' equally suitable for spiriting away or sublimating the actual limitations of their situation. What I claim is to live to the full the contradiction of my time, which may make sarcasm the condition of truth" (*Mythologies*, p. 12). After the fact, it is possible to see the extent to which the equation of semiology with structural analysis reduced the former to a bookish practice. Semiology was a powerful methodology beyond its potential application for textual analysis, extending to the study of culture and the life of signs in society described in Saussure's *Course* as the domain of semiology. Thus it was that what Jonathan Culler called the pursuit of signs opened onto an experiential dimension with direct ties to current inquiries into postmodernity.

Among those who contributed to the Parisian structuralism of the 1960s, Barthes's pivotal role is enhanced by a personal myth which is nothing less than disarming. More than any of his peers, Barthes made his critical practice unabashedly self-reflexive. In so doing, he returned consistently to the underlying questions of value and interpretation that the scientific ambitions of structural analysis had displaced. Barthes's assertion of the personal stake in critical inquiry scandalized those of his readers for whom he had embodied the triumph of linguistic and textual analyses over conventional practices which used the life of the author to explicate his or her writings. At the same time, those early supporters who reacted against what they saw as Barthes's turn away from the Parisian semiology of the 1960s failed to see that his progression had only extended the literary application of structural analysis to its logical extreme. If *S/Z* did not break fully with structural analysis, it marked at least a critical pause.

The misgivings that Barthes expressed at the start of *Mythologies* were much more than a personal disclaimer set apart from the central project of his semiology. Instead, the claim to live in full the contradiction of his time was a precondition of Barthes's critical practice. It located his approach to the study of signs within a postwar generation of left-wing intellectuals in France who hoped that "the gulf between the alienated intellectual and the 'real' world could be rendered meaningful and, miraculously, at the same time be made to disappear."[8] Today, the resurgence of interest in cultural studies derives in large part from revised forms of the critical model in the *Mythologies*.

Writing Signs/Writing Culture

Each of the eight essays in the present volume elaborates and comments on a specific element in the evolution of Barthes's study of signs. Organization of the book into three sections is meant to express the interplay of language and writing as the ethics of form Barthes first described in *Writing Degree Zero* (1953). Each essay is an excursus in the form of an exercise *à partir de* Barthes, beginning with or moving outward from his writings. Whatever homage or commemoration this gesture entails is secondary to the self-consciousness and reflexive practice of writing which Barthes's writing illustrates beyond its explicit content. Gary Shapiro explores how the philosophical content of Barthes's writings extends an intellectual tradition which draws heavily

from the example of Friedrich Nietzsche. But rather than point-
ing to a consistent vision on which one might confer the status
or prestige of a philosophy, Shapiro transposes the question of
what philosophy is or might be into the more personalized formulation of what it is *for Barthes*. Shapiro argues convincingly
that Barthes's texts illustrate a relation to the philosophical tradition represented by Plato, Descartes, Hegel, Nietzsche, Husserl,
and Sartre. At the same time, Barthes's later writings temper the
project of elucidating the founding precepts and doctrines associated with Western metaphysics by a more personalized sense
of the textual corpus as a writerly body traversed by cultural
codes, especially those of knowledge. The result is a relation to
philosophy that replaces analysis and explanation with a fragmentary writing practice visible notably in *Roland Barthes by
Roland Barthes* and *Camera Lucida*.

Shapiro's reading straddles the history of Western philosophy and a narrative staging, Barthes's recognition of a truth that
is markedly personal. The return to phenomenology invoked
in *Camera Lucida* marks a regression only in a limited sense, as
Barthes reconsiders what he might formerly have overlooked in
phenomenology that could provide him with an access to truth
capable of contending with emotion in real terms. The return is
thus motivated by the critical project that Barthes undertakes to
achieve through it. At the same time, Shapiro notes how the Winter Garden photograph of the mother as child found shortly after
her death elicits an emotional response on his part which he
transposes into concepts and an idiom for which phenomenology
strikes him as singularly appropriate.

Richard Howard uses anecdote and remembrance to add to
the mythic figure of Barthes set forth by Shapiro. In so doing, he
collapses the easy distinction between life and text into an ongoing field of semiosis and meaning. Appropriately, Howard's gesture is personal and openly mimetic: his supplement to Barthes's
own remarks—in *The Pleasure of the Text* and *Roland Barthes*—on
who Nietzsche is . . . *for him*. The same sense of imitation also in-
spires Mary Lydon, Lori Woodruff, and Susan Warren to stage
their collective memorial as a pedagogical performance mixing
knowledge, authority, and desire.

In "System vs. Code: A Semiologist's Etymology," Jean-Jacques

Thomas provides an alternative means of attaining the origin and truth of writing that Barthes hoped to illustrate by means of the "true" novel he planned to write out of his own life. Astutely, Thomas locates that means in a conceptual distinction between system and code. But where other commentators have noted the reflexive element in Barthes's writings after *S/Z* (1970), Thomas argues that Barthes's project of establishing a science of literature on rational description and explanation includes an element of reflexivity that is already evident in Barthes's mid-1960s practice of structural analysis. In such terms, what others have taken for Barthes's progression from science to writing is collapsed into a more unstable and problematic practice of writing within science.

Antoine Compagnon implicitly follows Thomas in "The Two Barthes" when he asserts that the inquiry based on a will to truth and origin leads inevitably to a split between one Barthes who studies the literary institution and another who studies literary creation. Thus, Compagnon notes the timeliness of reassessing the history of literary theory which Barthes had polemicized by setting structural analysis against a practice modeled in large part on Gustave Lanson's 1898 *History of French Literature* (*Histoire de la littérature française*).

Betty R. McGraw applies what Compagnon terms the "omission" (*impensé*) to analyze the striking parallels between the progression of Barthes's confessional writings—namely, *Roland Barthes by Roland Barthes*, *A Lover's Discourse*, and *Camera Lucida*—and Jean-Paul Sartre's 1938 novel, *Nausea*. For McGraw, the "omission" is meaningful as a sensation of ennui, a term whose usual translation into English as boredom misses the complexity of a personalized attitude toward time and existence which Sartre's early novel evokes with singular force. Like Sartre's narrator, Antoine Roquentin, Barthes uses the diary as a narrative form which breaks down time into discrete entities while it illustrates the inability of language to account for the shapelessness of human existence. At the same time, the comparison with the early Sartre allows McGraw to explore Barthes's return to an idiom of phenomenology which he had seemingly abandoned after his conversion to structural analysis in the 1950s. Simulating Barthes's use of fragmentary writing in her own text, McGraw also notes how Barthes's later writings constitute a unique self-analysis which hovers consistently between confession and dissimulation. The result is an original reading which approaches the connection with Sartre from the angle of confessional narrative.

Mary Lydon's refusal to separate literary from nonliterary texts extends Barthes's own progression beyond distinctions of genre toward what he terms writing as an intransitive verb.[9] Her gesture also recalls other problematic distinctions: namely, Jean-Jacques Thomas's discussion of the relationship between system and code, and Antoine Compagnon's denunciation of the split between literary institution and creation. "Happening on" suggestive *coincidences* while reading *Camera Lucida* and Freud's "A Case of Paranoia Running Counter to the Psychoanalytical Theory of the Disease," Lydon explores how the Barthes text resonates within the Freudian soundbox. Consonant with Barthes's use of personal value to challenge the claims of an omniscient truth, she notes how the *mathesis singularis* of Barthes's critical writing turns *Camera Lucida* into "an elaborate spectacle of sound and light: a spectacle ingeniously, if unconsciously, contrived at once to mourn the mother and to stage whatever conflicting feelings of culpability and fealty her image may have inspired in her devoted son." Her reading of the photograph of the mother as child in the Winter Garden (which she astutely renames the "conservatory") and of Freud's interpretation of his paranoid patient brings together a number of disparate elements: the abrupt click of the camera shutter, the throb of a desiring body, the "snapping" shut of the lid of the mother's *poudrier* (powder box), the formidable end-stops of Schumann's seventh *Kreisleriana*, and the spectral *Mutterbild* in the diminutive mirror in the compact case, the "luminous shadow" of the mother throughout *Camera Lucida*, and the hallucinatory power of Freud's patient triggered by her auditory delusion.

For Lydon, the photograph by Daniel Boudinet at the start of *Camera Lucida* constitutes a pendant to Barthes's essay. The photo is immediately striking because it is the only colored reproduction in the book. Moreover, she sees it as articulating with the Winter Garden photo that is not reproduced. The absent image of the mother in the Winter Garden is doubly *illuminating* insofar as it insists on the effects of the signifier and the delirium of interpretation within what Lydon studies in the contrapuntal play of sound and sight. Her conclusion—that "there is method in its madness"—invites the reader to seek out the effects of other coincidences by following her own interpretative intuitiveness to its logical conclusion.

The reflexive component in Barthes attains explicit expression in Lawrence D. Kritzman's "The Discourse of Desire and the Question of Gender" as the earlier analyses of confessional narrative and fiction are transposed into the standard concepts of psychoanalysis. Following the protocol of Barthes's later practice, Kritzman moves beyond the scientific ambitions of structural analysis toward a more personal knowledge that spans the divide between science and the senses. As Barthes might have put it, the progression is one from a claim to objective knowledge (*savoir*) toward something more subjective (*saveur*). Kritzman confronts the question of gender as it is set forth in what he terms Barthes's allegory of the discourse of desire. Among the forms of this allegory, he notes in particular how the law of gender determination produces the female body as semiotic object in Erté's alphabet of costumed women. Inasmuch as Kritzman also explores the neutralization of sexual difference in Barthes's equation of femininity and writing, he uses the latter's analysis of Brillat-Savarin's *Physiologie du goût* against Erté's attempt to desexualize the female body in order instead to underline the libidinal economy of the semiotic.

The question of gender is also pertinent to Kritzman's own narrativity. For in focusing on Barthes's "voluptuousness of vowels," Kritzman's affective investment reveals itself through a signifying practice which integrates Barthes's own sensuality. By describing Barthes's narrativity as alternately "cruising," "narcissistic," "symbiotic," "seductive," "clandestine," and "transvestite," Kritzman's own discourse reflects an image reminiscent of the Lacanian mirror phase insofar as the reader participates in the making of the textual body (*corpus*). Barthes's commentary on his own writing aptly describes Kritzman's euphoric narrative: "In him the desire for the word prevails, but this pleasure is partly constituted by a kind of doctrinal vibration" (*Roland Barthes by Roland Barthes*, p. 74). Kritzman's discursive performance is matched only by his subject; his juggling of words is nothing other than a *tour de force* that shows a paradisiac and symbiotic relationship between subject and object, in the best tradition of classical scholarship.

Where Kritzman analyzes the cultural debates surrounding representation of the primitive, Steven Ungar focuses instead on the primal and on what he sees as a persistence of the image in Barthes's writings on photography and film. What he maintains as Barthes's resistance to film entails an expansion of Barthes's practice of semiotics to include analysis of how certain photographs prefigure an involvement with film that he finds poignant—that is, problematic and disturbing. The reasons for this turn out to engage both an ongoing assessment of the semiotic project and an approach to the image that can be retraced in conjunction with the works of S. M. Eisenstein, Jean-Paul Sartre, André Bazin, and Christian Metz. A final illustration of Barthes's encounter with the image occurs in the scene of personal recognition staged in the meditation on the Winter Garden photo in *Camera Lucida*.

A number of historical concerns have contributed to the current collection. For those of us who came to study French literature some twenty to twenty-five years ago, one change of particular note began with the mid-1960s polemic between a young and relatively known critic—Barthes—on one side, and the late literary historian and Sorbonnard Raymond Picard. At the time, we did not fully understand why many of our teachers perceived structural analysis as a threat or why they ridiculed its vocabulary. Our reaction was a mixture of curiosity and mischief. But if the New French Criticism (*la nouvelle critique*) was riling our professional elders and forcing them to defend their practices as teachers and scholars, it was clearly something worthy of closer attention. What we found at first was less of a doctrine or a fully formed method than a set of reading practices derived from philosophy (most of it French and German), linguistics, and anthropology. Immediate changes were visible in the vocabulary: signs replaced words, texts displaced works. Suddenly—or so it seemed at the time—meaning was less a product of definition or authorial intention than of what came to be known as textuality and a practice of reading that is well characterized by Umberto Eco's notion of the open work (*opera aperta*). It is this openness—of possible meanings to be considered rather than of a mere plurality—that we hope to convey as the singular contribution that Barthes's writings have made to the study of signs in culture.

Notes

1. Ferdinand de Saussure, *Course in General Linguistics*, trans. Wade Baskin (New York: Philosophical Library, 1959), p. 16. The *Course* is, in fact, a posthumous work commonly attributed to Saussure but edited after Saussure's death in 1913 by Charles Bally and Albert Sechehaye on the basis of notes taken by students who attended Saussure's general course between 1906 and 1911. The issue of authorship and the belated discovery of Saussure's unpublished study of anagrams in late Roman poetry have led to a revised understanding of the *Course* and its status.

2. See Umberto Eco, *Theory of Semiotics* (Bloomington: Indiana University Press, 1976); Terence Hawkes, *Structuralism and Semiotics* (Berkeley: University of California Press, 1977); and Kaja Silverman, *The Subject of Semiotics* (New York: Oxford University Press, 1983). Alternative assessments abound; see, for example, Rosalind Coward and John Ellis, *Language and Materialism* (Boston: Routledge and Kegan Paul, 1977); Josué V. Harari, ed., *Textual Strategies* (Ithaca: Cornell University Press, 1979); Terry Eagleton, *Literary Theory: An Introduction* (Minneapolis: University of Minnesota Press, 1983); and Teresa de Lauretis, *Alice Doesn't: Feminism, Semiotics, Cinema* (Bloomington: Indiana University Press, 1984).

3. Jonathan Culler, *Ferdinand de Saussure* (New York: Penguin, 1976), p. 30.

4. Fredric Jameson, *The Prison-House of Language: A Critical Account of Structuralism and Russian Formalism* (Princeton: Princeton University Press, 1972), p. 18.

5. D. S. Clarke, Jr., *Principles of the Semiotic* (New York: Routledge and Kegan Paul, 1987), p. 30. Georges Mounin levels a similar charge against Barthes in *Introduction à la sémiologie* (Paris: Minuit, 1970), p. 194.

6. Roland Barthes. *Mythologies*, trans. Annette Lavers (New York: Hill and Wang, 1972), p. 11.

7. Barthes. "Inaugural Lecture," trans. Richard Howard, in Susan Sontag, ed., *A Barthes Reader* (New York: Hill and Wang, 1982), pp. 474–475.

8. Dick Hebdige, *Subculture: The Meaning of Style* (New York: Methuen, 1979), p. 10.

9. See Roland Barthes, "To Write: An Intransitive Verb?" in Richard Macksey and Eugenio Donato, eds., *The Languages of Criticism and the Sciences of Man: The Structuralist Controversy* (Baltimore: Johns Hopkins University Press, 1970), pp. 134–145. The paper was first read in October 1966 at the Johns Hopkins Humanities Center. It is reprinted in *The Rustle of Language*, trans. Richard Howard (New York: Hill and Wang, 1986), pp. 11–21.

Signs

of

Life and Death

PHILOSOPHY AND FRIENDSHIP

GARY SHAPIRO   "To Philosophize Is to
                Learn to Die"

---

*In the course of my life I have often had the same
dream, appearing in different forms at different
times, but always saying the same thing, "Socrates, practice and cultivate the arts." In the past I
used to think that it was impelling me and exhort-
ing me to do what I was actually doing: I mean
that the dream, like a spectator encouraging a
runner in a race, was urging me on to do what
I was doing already, that is, practicing the arts,
because philosophy is the greatest of the arts, and
I was practicing it. But ever since my trial, while
the festival of the god has been delaying my exe-
cution, I have felt that it might be this popular
form of art that the dream intended me to practice, in which case I ought to practice it and not
disobey.*   —Socrates, in Plato's *Phaedo*, 61*

As the quintessential man of letters, Roland Barthes had the genial gift of being able to sympathize with an endless variety of
discourses, texts, myths, and semiotic systems. The profusion of
apparent subjects—Japan, Brecht, Balzac, photography, "mythologies," classical writing, the theater—is perhaps calculated to
provoke the purist who insists on the values of thoroughness and
well-grounded inquiry. At the same time, one would have to be
obtuse to fail to recognize the critical projects that animate the
many books, essays, and studies; these are explorations that put
into question the often closed and crabbed commitment of the
scholar or critic to the confines of what he or she knows in "proper"
serious fashion.

Barthes's *Empire of Signs* may stand as the emblem of his polemic with scholarship; it is an imaginary voyage, undertaken by a
traveler who deliberately eschews a knowledge of the language of
the country where he travels and dispenses with the apparatus—
extensive studies of history, literature, and culture—that the trav-

eling scholar typically employs to attain some simulacrum of the mastery that is comfortably taken for granted when one is "at home" with one's own specialty or *Fach*. Barthes's desire to slide over the surface of Japanese life is, however, tied to his attempt to suspend or, as the phenomenologists (to whom we shall return) would say, "bracket" the Western metaphysical commitment to the values of the center and interiority. Barthes proposes to contest these values and the binary categories of center/periphery and interior/exterior that they exemplify and reinforce. In attributing the Western taste for concentric cities with a full center to "the very movement of Western metaphysics, for which every center is the site of truth," his language comes surprisingly close to the philosophical thematics of Derrida and Deleuze.[1] We might be tempted to say that Barthes is an imaginary traveler in philosophy as well as in Japan. In fact, there are resonances of philosophy and its language(s) throughout Barthes's work, sometimes oblique, sometimes polemical, sometimes simply as part of a body of reference texts (as in *A Lover's Discourse*). The first book, *Writing Degree Zero*, is a sustained answer to Sartre's *What Is Literature?* while the last book, *Camera Lucida*, is dedicated to Sartre's *L'Imaginaire;* the names of Plato, Descartes, Hegel, Nietzsche, Husserl, and a bevy of more recent French philosophers play across Barthes's pages.

The questions that I wish to pose revolve around the elusive relation between Barthes's writing and philosophy. They could be elaborated in a series, beginning perhaps with the most simpleminded: does Barthes have a philosophy? Surely, such a question in a Barthesian text would be rewritten: does "Barthes"—who? and by what principle of identity?—"have"—what is the notion of ownership here?—"a philosophy"?—is philosophy to be construed as oriented toward a single more or less centered and coherent system? At the end of such a series of questions we might be asking for a nuanced account of the ways in which Barthes is tempted by philosophy, fears it, desires it, tentatively tries on its robes, analyzes its signs and myths, or inscribes it by citation, parody, or temporary adoption of this or that "position" in his own texts. The project of assembling the questions and interrogating the texts is a large one; but I have suggested already that Barthes is not to be thought of simply as either inside or outside of philosophy.

The philosophical tradition, imbricated as it is in our languages, in the protocols of rhetoric and semiology, in the very texture of our cities (as Barthes insists), is not to be easily overcome or rejected, although it may be displaced, deconstructed, or read differently. Barthes's most "personal" texts—*Roland Barthes by Roland Barthes* and *Camera Lucida*, for example—maintain a relationship with philosophy even while aiming at the qualities of the unique, the bodily, the fragmentary, and the aphoristic that are meant to challenge the hegemony of "the movement of Western metaphysics, for which every center is the site of truth." One might say that philosophy, no matter how de-idealized, is still part of the writer's body; it helps to constitute that writerly body traversed by so many learned and inherited codes. It is itself a code of sorts (an economy of philosophemes, Derrida would say), subject to the same law of repression and the return of the repressed as any other bodily tendency that might be the subject of attempts at exclusion or extirpation.

I propose to interrogate Barthes's oblique relation to philosophy in a text that both deliberately and adventitiously operates as a conclusion and précis of his work—*Camera Lucida*. Adventitiously, because the appearance of the book was followed so rapidly by his death. Deliberately, because Barthes concludes on the basis of his meditations and his reading of the photograph of his mother that "once she was dead I no longer had any reason to attune myself to the progress of the superior Life Force (the race, the species). My particularity could never again universalize itself (unless, utopically, by writing, whose project henceforth would become the unique goal of my life). From now on I could do no more than await my total, undialectical death" (*CL*, p. 29).[2]

The exception of writing from the waiting for death must strike us as peculiar, for to be sustained it would require a thorough separation between the public body and the private body. Not only would the reconciliation of particularity and universality through writing be a utopian enterprise; it would also seem that—without some support in what is here parodically called the "Life Force"—the wish to write would itself be fantastic and utopian. But this is to anticipate the result of a reading yet to be done. For the time being, we may remark several features of this passage and its context. The language is highly philosophical (although sometimes set off by parodic majuscule type): "particularity," "universalize," "undialectical," "Life Force." The thematics of death announced here can hardly be extricated from their articulation in Hegel, Heidegger, or Derrida. Significantly, Barthes's thoughts take this turn in relation to a subject which had appealed to him at various times as precisely that medium in which it might be possible to avoid the theoretical and the philosophical: photography.

Camera Lucida has been described as a fragmentary or aphoristic book. Certainly it is so in some respects, and the impression of a discrete writing is strengthened by the formal separation of the text into forty-eight numbered sections. The reader will also know, perhaps, Roland Barthes by Roland Barthes, which is not only aphoristic in form but reflectively comments on that form and its meaning. Like Camera Lucida, the earlier text is interspersed with photographs. Yet Camera Lucida is a narrative, even if its components can sometimes be read differentially as aphorisms. More specifically, it is the narrative of an ontological quest inviting comparison with a number of other narratives (those of Plato, Descartes, Hegel, and others). I shall read Camera Lucida then, at least initially, as a variation on the genre of ontological quest; such a reading will perhaps help to situate the specific strategies and concepts of the inquiry in relation to the discourses of philosophy. This is the kind of reading that will be necessary, for example, if we want to understand what Barthes is doing in employing the language of universals and particulars and in seeing what he might mean when he writes of awaiting his very own "undialectical death."

As in the case of Descartes's Meditations and Hegel's Phenomenology of Mind, Barthes's narrative is marked by a distinction between a naïve "I" who does not yet know where the journey will lead and a more knowledgeable, sophisticated "I" who has completed it. The difference in these personae is clear from the beginning; the Barthes who narrates begins by citing an experience with a photograph (of Napoleon's youngest brother, Jerome) which had already been forgotten by the remembered naïve Barthes. Only sometime later was he "overcome by an 'ontological' desire: I wanted to learn at all costs what photography was 'in itself'" (CL, p. 1). Photography, we eventually learn, must be understood in terms of forgetting/remembering; here already in the stage setting of the ontological quest we encounter an experience that will be remembered only later. The quest, then, seems to have two beginnings: the personal and forgotten beginning in which Barthes wonders at seeing eyes (Jerome's) that saw Napoleon, and a more conventional philosophical beginning which aims at formulating a definition or essence. This explicit double origin of the quest gives it a context which the standard Cartesian or Hegelian narrative tends to obscure: Descartes does not incorporate his own visionary dreams into the *Meditations*, but mentions only the general possibility that we might be dreaming; Hegel does not recount his tangled relations with Hölderlin and Schelling, but speaks of the dialectic of lordship and bondage. What is at stake here is the role of context and exemplar in the philosophical narrative.

The photograph is a concrete tie to the past; it tells us "that-has-been." To imagine the philosophical quest as marked by photographs, then, is to see it as situated and contextualized. Barthes's (later) memory of the photograph of Jerome itself plays the role of the photograph; it tells us that, despite the theoretical prejudice that the ontological desire is a universal human possibility, each quest which takes place under the sign of that desire has its origin in an *event*. Barthes explains the mutual implication of photograph and event:

> In the photograph, the event is never transcended for the sake of something else: the photographer always leads the corpus I need back to the body I see; it is the absolute particular, the sovereign contingency, matte and somehow stupid, the *This* (this photograph, and not Photography), in short, what Lacan calls the *Tuché*, the Occasion, the Encounter, the Real, in its indefatigable expression.
> (*CL*, p. 2)

The photograph, and so the quest associated with it, resists any reduction to being a mere example of something more general; it has an insistent *haecceity* (as Duns Scotus and Charles Peirce would say) that will give any narrative not only what Barthes once called "the effect of the real" but what he now, more majestically, terms "the Real." Since Barthes's narrative, like so much of philosophy, will take the form of a mnemonic search, we could say that the text begins by dislocating and complicating the usual assumptions of such memory excursions. That is, a memory which is unremembered at the time when one begins an inquiry is later seen to have played a significant role in the acquisition and interpretation of other memories (one might think here of the role of the primal scene in psychoanalysis).

It is the stubborn particularity of the photograph that leads Barthes into his first philosophical impasse. Conventional aesthetic categories seem totally external to photographs in a way that they are not to the products of traditional arts. And searching for a theoretical analysis in the writings of others is frustrating: "Each time I would read something about photography, I would think of some photograph I loved, and this made me furious" (CL, p. 2). Like the systematic doubt practiced by Descartes or the Hegelian "highway of despair," the initial attempts at understanding lead to confusion and aporia. But, as in those philosophical narratives, the way out of the impasse lies in radicalizing and heightening its tensions. Barthes now sees himself as torn between two voices: that of impersonal science which would ask him to bracket his personal taste/distaste and that of the naïve primitive who would indulge his own fascination with *his* "referent, the desired object, the beloved body." The voice of science is one that Barthes's reader has heard before. It declares: "What you are seeing here and what makes you suffer belongs to the category 'Amateur Photographs,' dealt with by a team of sociologists; nothing but the trace of a social protocol of integration, intended to reassert the Family, etc." (CL, p. 2). The voice is that of Barthes in *Mythologies*, analyzing the cultural imperialism of "The Family of Man."

This experience of self-division is itself a classical philosopheme associated with the theoretical quest; it typically deepens the search by displacing it from an external arena to an internal one. Such a change of direction from ostensibly impersonal scientific understanding to that of the self which sees itself inextricably involved in the undertaking might be called Oedipal or tragic; of course, Barthes will contest the traditional associations of these terms with their implications of the normalcy of the succession of generations and gender identity. (To understand his "undialectical death" we shall have to interrogate the philosophical use of the "example" of death.) But the alteration of standpoint can be used to good effect without assuming such baggage, as in Nietzsche's narrative *The Genealogy of Morals*, which at first purports to be a scientific inquiry into the origin of morality but eventually becomes an arena in which "we" inquirers must recognize our own involvement in the economics of good and evil, guilt and redemption. This Nietzschean model for Barthes's enterprise may be obscured by the fact that Barthes's praise for Nietzsche (in *Roland Barthes by Roland Barthes*) is for his mastery of the aphoristic form. But it is worth recalling because Nietzsche's way of dealing with the classical "Descartes to Hegel" type of philosophical narrative is not only the fragmentation of aphoristic praxis but the parodic story which displaces evolutionary tales of moral progress (as in *The Genealogy of Morals*), the presentation of a new type of moral-philosophical hero (*Zarathustra*), or the autobiographical account of the ascent to wisdom (*Ecce Homo*).

In his own key, and with his own tone, Barthes's engagement with philosophy is something like that; in recalling his rejection of the scientific voice, he marks the transition with Nietzsche's name, where Nietzsche is understood as one who philosophically empowers a certain kind of fiction: "I began to speak differently. It was better, once and for all, to make my protestation of singularity into a virtue—to try making what Nietzsche calls the 'ego's ancient sovereignty' into an heuristic principle" (*CL*, p. 3).

The narrating Barthes now sees that the "dilemma . . . corresponded to a discomfort I had always suffered from: the uneasiness of being a subject torn between two languages, one expressive, the other critical; and at the heart of this critical language between several discourses . . ." (*CL*, p. 3). The fiction of *Camera Lucida* will be that "I [Barthes] make myself the measure of photographic 'knowledge'" (*CL*, p. 4), but that "I" maintains a constant dialogue with the voices of philosophy and science. Each gesture of the inquiring "I," now engaged in what he describes as a personal phenomenological quest, corresponds to or parodies a stage in the reflection or meditation characteristic of the more classical philosophical narrative. As for "the measure" Barthes asks himself, "What does my body know of photography?" and replies with a division into the operation of photography, being the subject of a photograph, and looking at photographs.

Since Barthes is not even an amateur photographer, he excludes the praxis of photography from his inquiry. This exclusion of action is a form of *askesis* which helps Barthes to focus on his perspective as observer. Yet focusing is an act, and an act that we identify with the operation of the camera; in his own way, Barthes is producing a series of snapshots. For Barthes, the "emotion" or "essence" of the photographer's experience is unspeakable and unknowable, just as for us, his readers, the Winter Garden photograph must be invisible and unintelligible; everything connected with the reading and writing of *Camera Lucida* must then take place as the other side of an absence which can never be filled in. Already in the early stages of Barthes's narrative, then, we can set the story over against the traditional comprehensive claims made by the Cartesian/Hegelian *Bildungsroman* or voyage of discovery which moves from confusion to clarity, absence to presence; already the unspeakable and the unreadable accompany what at one level purports to be a continuous recollection, *"Life/Death:* the paradigm is reduced to a simple click, the one separating the initial pose from the final print" (*CL*, p. 38).

That is precisely the experience Barthes reports having as a *subject* of photography—that is, the sense that he has been transformed into an other, an object, that he has "become Total-Image, which is to say, Death in person" (*CL*, p. 5). *Camera Lucida*, of course, contains no photos of Barthes, unlike its predecessor, which was filled with them. The entire text, in a sense, is his snapshot as a writer. In acknowledging his liking for the sound, the click of the camera when being photographed, Barthes is perhaps expressing his artistic fraternity with the photographer. Writing, too, is a mechanism, involving distinctive operations and sounds, at the point of both composition and printing (does Barthes speak of the sound of the pen or the typewriter?).

Barthes has completed the *askesis* necessary for his quest-narrative first by eliminating himself as actor (he is no photographer), and then by noting that photography effectively eliminates him as subject (to be photographed is to be killed). It is just at this point that the text opens up in a new way. The residue of Barthes's photographic body is now the spectator with his "I like/I don't like" (another ominous binary of the *fort/da* type containing a moment of sentencing or exclusion). Simultaneously, graphically, there begins to appear the series of photographs which are the subject of Barthes's likes and of his commentaries. No photos, then, without "I like/I don't like." But the photos double the text in a new way: if (as we shall see) the message of the photo is "that-has-been" or death, then the living narrative of the quest, already doubled by its philosophical models, is now juxtaposed with a non-narrative series of photos. As the objects of Barthes's likes, they form, for us, an array of times, places, and subjects; they act as a dispersion or diffusion of the trajectory that leads the writer on at the same time that again, for us, they are necessary so that we can follow that trajectory. The *punctum/studium* binary that is said to characterize the photograph now comes to characterize the text in which the photographs are embedded. The discursive part of the text, the words, constitutes its *studium*, making contact with cultural codes and traditions; the continuity of the *studium* is disrupted at twenty-four points by the photographs, which demand a different sort of attention. Arresting the continuous reading of Barthes's narrative, they call for a lingering attention and form a series to be contrasted with the words of the text.

Barthes's narrative, then, is qualified and interrupted by the very photographs on which he comments, yet the narrative is never obliterated by the photographs. The counterpoint of image and text is also a counterpoint of tenses. According to Barthes, the tense of the photograph is "that-has-been"; each one conveys a simple past, something over and done with or, at the extreme, something dead. The discursive narrative, however, always suggests a process of thought that is in the making, one that invites a sympathetic participation or identification by the reader. The typical tenses of Barthes's narrative are the present ("So I make myself the measure of photographic 'knowledge'") or the imperfect ("I was glancing through an illustrated magazine"). Verbal language, it seems, will not coincide with the images; the presence of the narrator guarantees the continuity that is excluded by photography.

After the appearance of the photographer in the text, Barthes continues to describe his inquiry as phenomenological:

But it was a vague, casual, even cynical phenomenology, so readily did it agree to distort or to evade its principles according to the whim of my analysis. First of all, I did not escape, or try to escape, from a paradox: on the one hand the desire to give a name to photography's essence and then to sketch an eidetic science of the photographer; and on the other the intractable feeling that photography is essentially (a contradiction in terms) only contingency,

singularity, risk: my photographs would always participate, as Lyotard says, in "something or other" . . . (*CL*, p. 8)

At first, phenomenology was the alternative to a semiology
with scientific aspirations; where semiology would have legis-
lated an inquiry into cultural codes and their underlying institutions, phenomenology promised a way of focusing on the nuances
and texture of experience insofar as it is one's own. The move
from semiology to phenomenology would be a step back in terms
of Barthes's own career and in relation to the standard narrative
of twentieth-century French intellectual life, in which phenomenology is what is transcended by structuralism, which is transcended by deconstruction and genealogy, which are transcended
by . . . Later, Barthes will tell us that he lacks a future. One way of
enacting that lack is to abandon at the beginning of the intellectual story his own beginnings (in semiology) and to regress to
an earlier stage (phenomenology, whose paradigm is apparently
Sartre's *L'Imaginaire*) which had previously been the object of his
critique. But phenomenology is still too scientific. Barthes would
like to say that the *eidos* of the photograph is its singularity, but
this is no *eidos* at all. How might one "do phenomenology" while
retaining the singular and contingent? And Barthes adds in effect
a second question: how might one practice a phenomenology that
does not reduce the affective, emotional side of the experience of
photographs? "Classical phenomenology, the kind I had known in
my adolescence (and there has not been any other since), had
never, so far as I could remember, spoken of desire or mourning"
(*CL*, p. 8). Of course, a number of Husserl's disciples (Scheler,
Plessner) had attempted phenomenologies of the emotions, although one might regard their studies, like Sartre's *The Emotions: Outline of a Theory*, as nonclassical. In any case, what is
important for Barthes is not really the question of whether one
might have a phenomenology of "desire or grief," but whether
having such will require the surrender of the emotions themselves; Barthes protests at the very logic of the "question" or
"theme": "As *Spectator* I was interested in photography only for
'sentimental' reasons; I wanted to explore it not as a question (a
theme) but as a wound: I see, I feel, hence I notice, I observe, and I
think" (*CL*, p. 8).

Beginning with Barthes's heuristic adoption of the fiction of the ego (on Nietzsche's advice), he has been searching for the proper *arché* for his inquiry. We might now describe that still somewhat tentative *arché* by paraphrasing Descartes: I am wounded, therefore I think. This might appear to be a reversal of the Cartesian *cogito ergo sum*, but it is more of a gloss that could also be expressed with a Sartrean accent. Descartes, after all, had used the fact of his doubting in order to establish his existence (and, if we follow the course of the *Meditations*, even that *arché* remains provisional until it is validated, in *Meditation* III, by the demonstration of God's existence). Doubt was also a kind of wound or insufficiency that could throw one into a state of radical uncertainty and self-conflict, such that one might wonder, for example, whether one's everyday perceptions are nothing but images without referents. (Barthes will short-circuit Descartes's doubt about the referent by defining the photograph in terms of an ineluctable referentiality.) Sartre provides a link of sorts between Cartesian doubt and the Barthesian "I am wounded"; for Sartre, the *cogito* has the form "I am a lack" or "I am an absence." In Barthes, the wound will take the form of death, both one's own and others'. Each *punctum* in the photographs that he values will be "an accident that pricks me" and so reminds him of his own mortality.

It is upon the establishment of this (tentative) Cartesian/Sartrean *arché* that Barthes articulates the distinction *studium/punctum* that he calls his "rule." Descartes had done something similar in assuming, provisionally, that the success of the *cogito* allowed him to employ the rule that all of his ideas which were both clear and distinct were true. One might even see a formal analogy between clarity/*studium* (that which is clearly understood) and distinctness/*punctum* (that which has been articulated into specific points and details). Barthes does not explicitly formulate his rule, which might be stated this way: attend to those photographs which exhibit a *studium* that is transversed or transgressed by a *punctum*. The rule seems to embody that very duality between a search for the *eidos* and an examination of affective consciousness that Barthes had described as the difficulty of his "cynical phenomenology." In good Cartesian or Hegelian fashion, Barthes has transformed an apparent opposition in the subject matter into a reflective procedure of apprehension. Universality and singularity have been retained and reconciled by making them correlative aspects of a rule. Barthes puts the rule to good use, productively piling up a series of observations reminiscent of his earlier critical and semiological work. The rule itself resembles in a formal way the distinction of figure/ground employed by Gestalt psychology.

Barthes's application of the rule (recounted to us narratively and reflectively) shows him as capable of following the scientific discipline of phenomenology, as the various forms or contents that may be assumed by *studium* and *punctum* are surveyed, classified, and distinguished. The "unary" photograph without a *punctum* is isolated as a degenerate case. The consequences of the *studium* being coded and the *punctum* being uncoded are drawn out; for example, "the incapacity to name is a good symptom of disturbance" or "in order to see a photograph well, it is best to look away or close your eyes" (*CL*, p. 22). All of this is reported in the imperfect or the novelistic present because Barthes the narrator knows that it eventually became impossible to settle into the regularized critical routine of a phenomenology or semiology of photography. So the narrator knows that the scientific Barthes was really gathering his forces and collecting his experiences for a deeper inquiry into himself. The later, narrating Barthes can provide a psychoanalytic account of the (relatively) impersonal concerns of the earlier investigator who directed his phenomenological rule upon the photographs selected by his "I like/I don't like."

Barthes finally comes to criticize his own activity in using the rule precisely because it leads only to a series of observations, a "bad infinite" (as Hegel would say), and not to the definition which philosophy seeks for its object:

> Proceeding this way from photograph to photograph (to
> tell the truth, all of them public ones, up to now), I had
> perhaps learned how my desire worked, but I had not dis-
> covered the nature (the *eidos*) of photography. I had to
> grant that my pleasure was an imperfect mediator, and
> that a subjectivity reduced to its hedonist project could
> not recognize the universal. I would have to descend
> deeper into myself to find the evidence of photography,
> that thing which is seen by anyone looking at a photo-

graph and which distinguishes it in his eyes from any
other image. I would have to make my recantation, my
palinode. (*CL*, p. 24)

Would it be overly tendentious to suggest that his crucial
turning point in Barthes's narrative of himself as philosopher,
here a philosopher recalled by his conscience to the search for
universality, is a transformation of an analogous turn of Socrates
in the *Phaedrus*? There Socrates gives a speech about love that he
later recants on both moral and metaphysical grounds: on moral
grounds because the speech shamefully advocates that the beloved yield himself to the nonlover, for crassly utilitarian reasons;
on metaphysical grounds, because the speech does not determine
the essence or *eidos* of love. Stricken with shame, Socrates hides
his head and declares that he must now make up for his sins by
reciting a palinode which will be a true speech about love.

Now while love and desire are also the themes (so far) of
Camera Lucida, Barthes's self-reproach seems to involve a charge
of delay and temporization rather than one of outright moral
transgression. But Barthes's "first speech" (as recounted in *CL*,
pp. 1–23), like the one regretted and retracted by Socrates, is the
expression, as he says, of a "hedonist project" which must lead to
bad morals and bad metaphysics. The second part of Barthes's
text, then, will constitute the true voice of love and of the metaphysical quest. But Socrates' second speech will be rewritten, for
love's focus will be not on an ever-expanding totality (the love of
Beauty and the Forms), but will come to be defined in relation to
an absolutely determinate past; and truth will turn out to be
"undialectical."

Nevertheless, recollection will be the path common to Barthes
and the Platonic Socrates; yet the philosopheme of recollection
will mean something completely different when both its subject
and object are mortal bodies rather than the separable soul and
the pure objects of knowledge. Barthes then will be reinscribing
the love story of the philosophical tradition; not attempting the
impossible feat of rejecting it altogether, but of modifying its vocabulary, its mood, and its tone in accordance with the materiality of the body, the body's image, and the mechanism (photography) which functions as an artificial memory. Of course, it is

just this mechanism of artificial memory that is the other focus of attention in the *Phaedrus* itself. There writing is the *pharmakon* (undecidably gift, poison, drug, remedy) which immobilizes, kills, and preserves living speech and thought. We live in the graphic age of artificial memory (*hypomnesis*), including the omnipresence of the visual image, whether moving (film, television) or still (photo-graphy). To embrace the still photograph in preference to the film, a taste which Barthes confessed at the start of his journey (*CL*, p. 1), is to favor the graphic in its typical and minimal form, in which it makes no pretension to motion and life. Barthes did not know the grounds of this preference at the beginning, but he comes to learn them; for the same reason he excludes color from true photography later on (although *La chambre claire* is prefaced by a monochromatic, greenish Polaroid photo that is not reproduced in the English translation).

These considerations point to the particular register in which Barthes rewrites Socrates' palinode (it may be worth recalling that both the *Phaedrus* and the *Symposium* are among Barthes's reference texts in *A Lover's Discourse*). Socrates' ideal love story begins with a primal vision of eternal truth and beauty; but that vision is forgotten and (we would say) repressed with varying intensities in different individuals. But a form of mnemonic recapture of that metaphorical vision is available which begins with an apparently mundane visual event:

> But when a man recently initiated, who has looked upon
> many of the great realities, sees a god-like countenance or
> physical form the beauty of which is a faithful imitation
> of true beauty, a shudder runs through him and some-
> thing of the old awe steals over him. . . . Once he has re-
> ceived the emanation of beauty through his eyes, he grows
> warm, and through the perspiration that ensues he irri-
> gates the sprouting of his wing. (*Phaedrus*, 251)

Barthes's love story, in contrast, begins (that is, from the time that he initiates the search for his mother through her photographs) as a voluntary search for what is known in advance to be the specific and determinate; Socrates' begins with a particular vision of a beautiful person and leads, if successful, to a "dialectical" or totalizing love for beauty. What Barthes had originally sought in the story related in his palinode was not the visual image of his mother but the right stimulus to *write* about her:

> Now, one November evening shortly after my mother's death, I was going through some photographs. I had no hope of "finding" her, I expected nothing from these "photographs of a being before which one recalls less of that being than by merely thinking of him or her" (Proust). I had acknowledged that fatality, one of the most agonizing features of mourning, which decreed that however often I might consult such images, I could never recall her features (summon them up as a totality). No, what I wanted—as Valéry wanted, after his mother's death— was "to write a little compilation about her, just for myself" (perhaps I shall write it one day, so that, printed, her memory will last at least the time of my own notoriety). (*CL*, p. 25)

Barthes set out to produce one of those reminders to oneself which provoked the denunciation of the written word in the *Phaedrus* (and in the logocentric tradition of Western philosophy). Such artificial memory is said to be simply a recipe for forgetting. To the extent that the planned memoir might be read by others, it would be separated from its author, "the father of the *logos*"; it would be an orphan with no one to come to its aid in the event that it is questioned, misinterpreted, or abused. Barthes does not in fact write this memoir of his mother (unless we construe *Camera Lucida* as in fact being that text). Like her picture, it is for us what Derrida calls a "spectral referent." Instead, the act of poring over the family photographs leads, eventually, to a visionary encounter. But the way to the vision is not easy, for Barthes first notices how "History" separates him from his mother by dressing her in an unfamiliar costume and placing her in a different setting: "There is a kind of stupefaction in seeing a familiar being dressed *differently*" (*CL*, p. 26). Or we might describe the path to the vision as the easiest of all, because the end was not deliberately sought. For Barthes, the family photographs were initially technical objects, part of the project of artificial memory, and his attitude toward them repeats, in a different key, the fruitless classificatory activities with which his ontological quest for the *eidos* of the photograph had begun: "I could not even say that I loved them: I was not sitting down to contemplate them, I was not engulfing myself in them. I was sorting them, but none seemed to me really 'right'" (*CL*, p. 25).

Unlike the lover in Socrates' palinode, Barthes knows from the beginning that he is seeking to reactivate a memory, but this hypomnemonic search, based on the cataloguing of old photos, presents him with the question "did I *recognize* her? . . . I recognized her differentially, not essentially" (*CL*, p. 27). Barthes's account of the laborious "Sisyphean" process of "straining toward the essence" seems to invoke the difficulties of Platonic or Hegelian dialectic—that is, "the labor of the negative" (as Hegel called it), which is involved in the criticism of the various possible concepts or definitions of that which we seek to know.

It is while caught up in these labors that Barthes discovered the Winter Garden photograph that revealed to him then "the truth of the face I had loved" and, on reflection, the very *eidos* of photography. Of the "truth" that Barthes finds, there is not much to be said, since it is, as he repeatedly emphasizes, a truth peculiar and particular to him; it is, he tells us, her innocence and kindness. The isolation and uniqueness of this quality is suggested by the claim that it stands in no relation to circumstances or context: "In this little girl's image I saw the kindness which had formed her being immediately and forever, without her having inherited it from anyone; how could this kindness have proceeded from the imperfect parents who had loved her so badly—in short: from a family? Her kindness was specifically *out-of-play*, it belonged to no system . . ." (*CL*, p. 28).

This description of the truth of the photograph, and its position at the end of a search (a search whose end was not and could not have been clearly envisioned from the beginning) bears a certain resemblance to Socrates' account of what lies at the end of the lovers' quest. Having recognized the intimations of true beauty in and through each other, they continue their ascent when death releases them from the body. Borne aloft by their recently liquified wings, nourished by earthly beauty, they are able, finally, to attain a vision of that self-sufficient beauty: "Whole and unblemished also, steadfast and blissful were the spectacles we gazed at in the pure light of final revelation, pure initiates as we were . . ." (*Phaedrus*, 250). Plato and Socrates cannot *present* us with this beauty which depends on nothing else, which is only radiant and never receptive. There is no way an embodied soul can partake of a vision that earthly ocular experiences can anticipate only by metaphor. So we have an analogical series of approximations to both journey and goal, as in the Platonic dialogues and the myths embedded in them. Now, although the Winter Garden photograph of his mother is available and could be reproduced (a number of family photographs were printed earlier in *Roland Barthes by Roland Barthes*), Barthes does not reproduce it because "it exists only for me. For you, it would be nothing but an indifferent picture . . ." (*CL*, p. 30). It is unpresentable (to any but Barthes) for reasons just the opposite of those that make Platonic beauty unpresentable. Such a photograph demonstrates the possibility "utopically, [of] *the impossible science of the unique being*" (*CL*, p. 28).

Yet, while the Winter Garden photograph does not appear, another photograph occupies the place where we might expect to find it. In the midst of Barthes's discussion of his mother's photo the text exhibits Nadar's portrait of "his mother (or of his wife—no one knows for certain)" (*CL*, p. 28). The photograph by Nadar is a determinate displacement of the Winter Garden photograph. The latter is of a very young girl; the subject is identified (Barthes's book documents it as his mother), but the photographer is unknown. Nadar's subject is somewhat indeterminate (mother or wife?—and, if plausibly either of these, why not some other woman?), but the photographer is famous (Barthes reproduces three of his photographs and forthrightly declares that he judges him to be the world's greatest photographer). In all these respects the present(ed) photograph is the alternative to the absent one and so reinforces the sense of its absence. Barthes is about to announce that the essence of photography, which he discovered in this absent photograph, is just its inevitable pastness; its *noema* cannot be present but is always a form of absence: "*that-has-been*" (*CL*, p. 32).

Barthes's text here reverses Plato's, in the way that the Nadar photograph reverses the Winter Garden one. Plato, whose fictional Socrates criticizes writing, knows that he writes; his own text must escape the critique by showing how it is distinguished from and superior to the written speech of Socrates recited by Phaedrus. In that respect, the entire *Phaedrus* is a palinode that answers the criticism of writing it contains. But in order to construct such a palinode, Plato must make a gesture in the direction of effacing the characteristics of writing from the work. It must seem to be free-flowing, living speech; as it turns out, it is a dialogue that might easily be performed without showing the script to the audience, although the script of Lysias from which Phaedrus reads would indeed be in evidence as an object of ridicule and parody.

The machinery of Barthes's writing is out in the open. His text is divided into numbered sections, which force upon the reader the sense of spacing; like Nietzsche's aphoristic writing, these spaced, fragmented pages inhibit an idealizing tendency that would make the text a transparent presentation of a continuous, integrated body of thought. More pointedly (this is its *punctum*), the text is marked by the photographs of quite material (human) bodies. The contrast is not one that could be found in just any book of photographs. Color photographs, unlike these starkly black-and-white ones, might be used to create the impression of a continuous, well-integrated presentation. Like the orphan *logoi* whose fate is lamented by Socrates, these pictures appear in the text without benefit of paternal protection. The sense of the photograph is beyond the photographer's supervision; Barthes defines the *punctum* as a dimension of meaning that arises only because of the unnameable disturbance it provokes in a viewer. Whether the photographer intended this *punctum* seems irrelevant; the *punctum* must be mine (Barthes's *studium/punctum* distinction might be illuminated by thinking of it in terms of Heidegger's contrast of the existential modes of *das Man* and *Jemeinigkeit*). When Barthes characterizes the *punctum* as "what I add to the photograph and *what is nonetheless already there*" (*CL*, p. 23), this "*already there*" is not a function of an authorial intention but a feature of the constituted photographic text.

Barthes's book, then, is a kind of rewriting of the Platonic narrative in a space where the metaphysics of presence has been put into question. Love, desire, and discourse are rethought in terms of mechanism, an irreversible pastness, and a hesitation before all dialectical resolutions that would produce higher unities out of differences. We have just seen that the generation of meaning that occurs when Barthes reads photographs cannot be construed on the model of that infinitely open-ended dialogue that aims at the whole, the totality which would include all valid discourse. More poignant, perhaps, is the exclusion of eye-contact, which is for Plato the bodily analogue of the contact of souls through language. As Socrates tells it in his palinode, love begins with a vision of a beautiful other; in order for love to grow wings it is necessary that the other return my gaze and that a reciprocal communication of the eyes be initiated: "Just as wind or echo rebounds from smooth, hard surfaces and returns whence it came, so the stream of beauty flows back again into the beautiful beloved through his eyes, the natural inlet to the soul. There it comes and excites the soul, watering the outlets of the wings and quickening them to sprout; so in his turn the soul of the loved one is filled with love" (*Phaedrus*, 255).

But the photographed subject is not looking at anyone who is looking at the photograph. Because he is seen without seeing, he feels the gap between "himself" and his image: "Photography transformed subject into object . . ." (*CL*, p. 5). What makes photography distinctive is just this power of generating a look that meets no other look:

> That is the paradox: how can one have an *intelligent air* without thinking about anything intelligent, just by looking into this piece of black plastic? It is because the look, eliding the vision, seems held back by something interior. The lower-class boy who holds a newborn puppy against his cheek (Kertesz, 1928), looks into the lens with his sad, jealous, fearful eyes: what pitiable, lacerating pensiveness? In fact, he is looking at nothing; he *retains* within himself his love and his fear: that is the Look.
>
> Now the Look, if it insists (all the more, if it lasts, if it traverses, with the photograph, Time)—the Look is always potentially crazy: it is at once the effect of truth and the effect of madness. (*CL*, p. 46)

This observation, it might be noted, is accompanied on the facing page by a photograph of Mondrian staring frontally (crazily?) into the camera.

Barthes's most radical inversion of the Platonic story has to do with a transformation of the meaning of madness. For Plato and Barthes alike, the gifts of madness are to be contrasted with the banality of convention, yet in all other respects they part company. Platonic madness, the madness of love as philosophy, involves an opening up and exchange of looks that eventually leads to the common apprehension of that which is impersonal and independent of your look, my look, or our exchange of looks. The madness of photography, Barthes suggests, has to do with its absolute attachment to the particular. Photography can be tamed by making it into an art (arts are respectable and intelligible), or by its banalization in a gregarious sea of images (as in the United States, Barthes says), or it will be "mad if this realism is absolute and, so to speak, original, obliging the loving and terrified consciousness to return to the very letter of Time" (CL, p. 48).

What is the "very letter of Time"? It is the *noema* of photography, "that-has-been," a past that is fixed and separated from us. But because of this ineluctable pastness, the "very letter" is also death, if we are able to understand death in a rigorously undialectical way. This at least is what Barthes first claims to read in the Winter Garden photograph and then, on a larger scale, comes to understand in reading the place of photography within our culture. The first realization coincides with the attitude of the Greeks (the tragic and not the Platonic Greeks, we should add): they "entered into Death backward: what they had before them was their past" (CL, p. 29). And so Barthes, the observer of (his mother's) death, began looking at her more recent photographs and arrived finally at a vision of her as changed into herself. Here Barthes alludes to a poem of Mallarmé's that is simultaneously reminiscent of Hegel's principle that *Wesen ist was gewesen ist*. Essence is what has been or, in Barthes's phrase, "that-has-been." This reminiscence of one of the great thinkers of life and death should not appear arbitrary here, for it is just in connection with the discovery of the mother, and of photography's essential connection with death, that Barthes confronts the philosophical tradition with his experience of photography:

> If, as so many philosophers have said, Death is the harsh victory of the race, if the particular dies for the satisfaction of the universal, if after having been reproduced as other than himself, the individual dies, having thereby denied and transcended himself, I who had not procreated, I had, in her very illness, engendered my mother. Once she

was dead I no longer had any reason to attune myself to the progress of the superior Life Force (the race, the species). My particularity could never again universalize itself (unless utopically, by writing, whose project henceforth would become the unique goal of my life). From now on I could do no more than await my total undialectical death. (*CL*, p. 29)

The philosophical thought that Barthes summarizes here is indeed classical. For both Plato and Aristotle, the reproduction of the species is the normal way of achieving a kind of immortality (more difficult ways involve the production of immortal works or attaining a philosophical contemplation of the eternal). Tragedy turns on the fact that these forms of immortality are highly fragile and that the different forms may interfere with one another. So on Aristotle's analysis it is Oedipus, the man of knowledge, who, ignorant of his own parentage, begets children who must also be the end of his line of generation. But normally death is dialectical in the sense that the individual is negated and transcended by the species. It is Hegel (from whom, ultimately, Barthes borrows this language of universality, particularity, negation, and transcendence) who formulated the principle that the child is the death of its parents. But if there is no transcendence through the begetting of another generation, then death is undialectical. In the metaphysical tradition that links Plato to Hegel, the possibility of a particular failure to participate in the dialectical process is always recognized. Hence tragedy, which plays in the gap between the ideal and the actual. Yet tragedy reinforces the ideal because its failures are unintelligible without it.

Despite Barthes's having opened the philosophical passage above with a reference to the Greeks, we might understand him as substituting the very modern cultural fact of photography for the traditional art of tragedy. The substitution supposes that there is indeed a place to be filled. On the one hand, Barthes has explicitly undertaken the philosophical quest for the *eidos* of what we may call an art (despite his reservations about the normalizing tendency of that designation). On the other, it could be noted that the philosophical quest, because of the way in which it requires narrative, must exist in uneasy relationship with those arts or forms of storytelling whose claims to truthfulness it would like to dismiss. Photography is what tragedy becomes when life and death are thought nondialectically.

Here Barthes joins forces with the anti-Hegelian movement of recent French thought. Hegel takes tragedy (and to some extent comedy) to be the most philosophical of arts, by which death and conflict are given a *meaning*. *Antigone*, Hegel's choice as the greatest tragedy and greatest work of art, can be given a detailed structural and dialectical analysis, as in the *Phenomenology of Spirit*, in which it is shown that death is intelligible as the only possible intersection of the worlds of men and women (at least in a society like early Greece that thinks of natural distinctions as equivalent to cultural categories).[3] But for Barthes the photograph is an unvarnished intrusion of death: ". . . if dialectic is that thought which masters the corruptible and converts the negation of death into the power to work, then the photograph is undialectical: it is a denatured theater where death cannot 'be contemplated,' reflected and interiorized; or again: the dead theater of Death, the foreclosure of the Tragic, excludes all purification, all *catharsis*" (*CL*, p. 37).

The life of spirit, Hegel had said, grandly and ambitiously, "is not the life that shrinks from death and keeps itself untouched by devastation, but rather the life that endures it and maintains itself in it. It wins its truth only when, in utter dismemberment, it finds itself."[4] But where, in our culture, can we find an art or activity that acknowledges and surmounts death in this way? Have we, perhaps, already witnessed the death of tragedy? Isn't that death part of the same movement that has called into question both the pantragic, dialectical conception of history and the dialectical interpretation of artistic and cultural forms? Yet Barthes still will insist, despite such changes, that "death must be somewhere in a society." Our form of death is a "flat" one, purged of teleological narrative, of religion, and of ritual: "*Life/Death:* the paradigm is reduced to a simple click, the one separating the initial pose from the final print" (*CL*, p. 38). The earliest works of art in Hegel's grand narrative, the *Lectures on Aesthetics*, are the monuments, designed to immortalize, which were erected by the Egyptians and Indians. Now, Barthes observes, we have renounced the monument and have replaced it with the "flat death" of photography.

But photography is not simply *about* death. The Cartesian turn taken by Barthes's inquiry when he decided (provisionally) to adopt the standpoint of the ego has now become a Heideggerian insistence on the ineluctability of his own death. Thinking of the Winter Garden photograph from which he derives the essence of photography, Barthes finds that it "says" very little and so he cannot penetrate to its heart or transform it into philosophical or critical discourse (his criticism and his philosophy will be concerned with this very lack). But, he adds, "The only 'thought' I can have is that at the end of this first death, my own death is inscribed; between the two, nothing more than waiting" (*CL*, p. 38). It is as if both the cultural *studium* of Barthes's text and the *punctum* of the photographs that accentuate and interrupt it tend toward the impossible speech act "I am dead" that Barthes had explored in Poe and Derrida had found implicit in Husserlian phenomenology. As the latter suggests in his meditation on the insistently indexical character of the sign: "The appearing of the *I* to itself in the *I am* is thus originally a relation with its own possible disappearance. Therefore *I am* originally means *I am mortal.*"[5] That is what Barthes discovers in photography, and it is a discovery that both deepens and renders irreversible the experiment of undertaking a subjective approach that he had embarked upon under the sign of Nietzsche.

It is, then, perhaps more than a coincidence that Barthes's concluding rhapsody in his palinode in praise of photographic madness again appeals to Nietzsche's example. This time, however, it is not the cool Nietzsche who inventively suggests new procedures and methods of inquiry, but the mad Nietzsche who is the (Dionysian) victim of a scandalous love. The love awakened by the photograph, Barthes confesses, resounds with the music of pity (the temptation against which Nietzsche argued and thought). In the photographs that he loved, Barthes now sees, "I passed beyond the unreality of the thing represented, I entered crazily into the spectacle, into the image, taking into my arms what is dead, what is going to die, as Nietzsche did when, as Podach tells us, on January 3, 1889, he threw himself in tears on the neck of a beaten horse: gone mad for Pity's sake" (*CL*, p. 47).

In this text so replete with philosophical citations and allusions (I have only been able to indicate a portion of its philosophical economy), why is the final philosophical snapshot devoted to the madness of Nietzsche? No doubt the reference is overdetermined. Nietzsche appeared first to authorize a kind of experimental phenomenology; he reappeared in the palinode to confirm the significance that Barthes accords to the Winter Garden photograph: "All the world's photographs formed a Labyrinth. I knew that at the center of this Labyrinth I would find nothing but this sole picture, fulfilling Nietzsche's prophecy 'A labyrinthine man never seeks the truth, but only his Ariadne'" (CL, p. 73).

We recall that Ariadne herself was not at the center of the labyrinth but supplied the thread which allowed the explorer to map its penetralia and return to the point of entrance. Barthes confirms this by explaining that the prized photograph was not the key to a "secret thing (monster or treasure)" but invaluable for its power to "tell me what constituted that thread which drew me toward photography" (CL, p. 30). Beyond truth, then, there is the madness of love; but that love must be understood in relation to a pre-Platonic myth that valorizes the specific person who is its object and that, rather than opening out into the cosmic spaces of the eternal forms, is set in a very complex interior, in a cave lacking the illumination of the sun. We remember that Barthes's discovery occurs at night, at home, in the dark time of the year, by the artificial illumination of a lamp. If Barthes wishes to construct an anti-Platonic palinode, then Nietzschean madness will substitute for the *mania* praised by Socrates. The madness of love for the absolute particular replaces that of the lovers who transcend the visually beautiful. Perhaps we shall think, too, of the contrast between the despised, beaten work horse of Turin and the team of horses (one noble, one base) driven by the soul in the Platonic myth. The possibility is reinforced by the Kertesz photograph of a young boy with a small puppy that appears on the page opposite the prose section where Barthes cites Nietzsche's episode with the horse.

Socrates concludes his palinode by enumerating the benefits of that philosophical pursuit which is the gift of a certain kind of madness. If Barthes brings his to an end by remembering Nietzsche's collapse, it is both to suggest a different form of madness and perhaps to situate the madness of photography within our age. If Barthes is not only constructing a palinode but also narrating the story of his philosophical quest, then we should not be surprised to find that that narrative, like all of its classical philosophical predecessors, must include a history of philosophy itself. In the largest and most ambitious metanarrative of philosophy's history, that is, Heidegger's story, the Western obsession with presence (a kind of madness or *hybris*) is bounded by the figures of Plato and Nietzsche. What begins with the Platonic attempt to discern the possibility of total presence in the ideality of the forms ends with Nietzsche's celebration of the will to power, conceived as a generalization of what is taken to be most pressingly present to us subjectively or personally.

In this Heideggerian story, Nietzsche's final madness is emblematic of the madness (a grand, tragic, heroic madness no doubt) which has animated philosophy since Plato. Much depends on the question of whether such a metanarrative of philosophy's history can be established and maintained. To the extent that it can be, the individual philosophical quest can be anchored in a story with a beginning, a middle, and an end (Plato, Descartes, Nietzsche—for example). But suppose that Nietzsche is to be recast, to follow the letter and image of Barthes's text, as the philosopher of the photographic epoch and its madness. Would the story then be skewed, interrupted, and deprived of its closure? If death is present in our culture by means of photography, then perhaps Nietzsche is the thinker of that kind of death, the thinker of the century that, as Barthes tells us, paradoxically invented both photography and history (*CL*, p. 38). This madness, the philosophical madness that would replace Platonic-dialectical madness, would join death and historicity with the specificity of "that-has-been." Perhaps we can hear some of that madness in Zarathustra's fragments of a lover's discourse that appear under the title "The Tomb Song":

> O you visions and apparitions! O all you glances [*Blicke*] of love, you divine moments [*Augenblicke*]! How quickly you died. Today I recall you as my dead ones. From you, my dearest friends among the dead, a sweet scent comes to me, loosening heart and tears . . . I must now call you after your disloyalty, you divine glances and moments: I have not yet learned any other name. Verily, you have died too soon for me, you fugitives. Yet you did not flee from me, nor did I flee from you: we are equally innocent in our disloyalty.[6]

Zarathustra grieves for the divine moment, for the *Augenblick*—literally the blink of an eye, the time that it takes to capture a snapshot of experience and to transform it into a memory. In the blinking of the eye, can we hear this sound of the camera? "*Life/Death*: the paradigm is reduced to a simple click, the one separating the initial pose from the final print" (*CL*, p. 92). The other, equally mad side of this love of the dead and entombed moment is called the thought of eternal recurrence. But in "The Tomb Song," which is not yet able to speak (or sing) that thought, we see death generalized, deprived of any ritual and religion other than that which consists in reviewing the snapshots or blinkings of the eye that are the traces of the dead.

"To philosophize is to learn to die." Barthes had supposed that he was engaged in a philosophical quest for the *eidos* of photography. He had read philosophy (and everything else) and had become a writer, a critic, a teacher, a *moraliste;* but never before had he set out to "do philosophy," that is, to construct a method and to articulate a set of categories from the ground up. He began by noting, like Descartes, the paucity of the literary and critical resources—that is, the various rhetorical and empirical classifications of photography; but the idea of continuing along the lines of a "pure" phenomenology (that is, one independent of the inquirer's personal situation and a textual tradition) collapses almost as soon as it is formulated. Doing philosophy becomes not the hedonistic project assumed in the ode but the meditation on love and death of the palinode. But in the photographic age the classical formula of Socrates and Montaigne must be rethought and reinscribed. It is not simply traditional wisdom that Barthes acquires and displays through his confessional narrative and the photographs in the text. As Derrida suggested in the case of Husserl, death is no longer to be conceived as an isolated narrative event, but as the ineluctable accompaniment of every "I am." It is as if we were to rewrite Kant's thesis "the 'I think' must be able to accompany every act of consciousness" by substituting an "I am mortal" for the *cogito*. This new form of the "I think" must be both unique and absolutely general. It is as available as the family book of photographs.

It is this pluralizing power of Barthes's deaths and of his dead (ones) that is articulated in Derrida's essay "Les morts de

Roland Barthes."[7] One might describe this reading of death as a death announcement by postcard: Barthes supplies pictures and text, while we are, if not the addressees, at least its recipients. The letter that bears the news of death is no longer delivered in a black-bordered envelope by special messenger; it may turn up in the magazine or newspaper. But who reads, who receives, these letters? Are the readers the "proper" recipients or does a certain chance come into play in both receipt and reading? Surely in construing *Camera Lucida* as a being engaged with the question of how one "does philosophy" I have assimilated it all too easily to the cultural *studium* of my professional activity, even if I have accented it by the *punctum* of a more specific and personal interest in certain texts of Plato, Hegel, or Nietzsche. Not having known Barthes outside of his texts, having never met him or heard him lecture, I am freed in a certain way to take up his postcards as I choose. In any case, I continue to read Barthes, especially the texts that I have not read before, and so he remains on my horizon; in a certain sense he is still alive, for me.

While writing this essay, word came to me of the death of my Uncle Byron. I don't have the right picture of Bye and there would be no point in showing it if I had. I hadn't seen him for over a dozen years, since my father's funeral. The death of the uncle, the last and youngest of three brothers, ought, on the basis of Barthes's meditations on genealogy and dialectics, to force me finally to think of myself as part of the older generation with a responsibility for family tradition (news, gossip) and ritual. Unlike Barthes, I've married and fathered children, so my death could be tempered by dialectics, *aufgehoben* in the continuity of family or race, and I could, in good conscience, make common cause with a Hegelian philosophy of historical teleology (with suitable modifications by Kojève or Sartre). But Barthes's deaths are also deaths of and for that *studium*, philosophy, which, as he reminds us, has never really been far from death.

What I recall most about Uncle Bye was his introducing me, along with a small army of cousins, to the ritual and mystery of the movies. His occupation allowed him to produce private showings on the birthdays of some of us children (and once he even saw to it that I met one of my favorite stars). In that projection-studio one saw the praxis of showing the movie; Bye could choose what was to be shown, decide when the lights were to go off or on, set the stage. The movies in this form gave us a feeling of participating in a festive ritual, presided over by the kindly uncle who could arrange the entire scene with his wizardly powers. At that time I didn't ask what the movies were—that is, I didn't wonder about their *eidos*. When I came to think of myself as a philosopher, it was literature in its print and its solitude that I thought one might try to understand someday. Barthes distinguished photography from the cinema, perhaps because the latter nourishes a certain image of continuous narrative; certainly it can be a form of normalizing and domesticating the mad possibilities of photography. Of course, there are other possibilities, including, most obviously, the introduction of the *punctum* of the still photograph into the moving *studium* of the film. In *Blow-Up* or *Under Fire* the device is used in connection with deaths that are either captured or foreshadowed by the click and whir of the camera.

So now I have suffered a kind of interruption with the death of that uncle who initiated me into the culture of the movies. My memories will be punctuated, my faith in Aristotelian or Hegelian stories subject to new forms of interrogation. Perhaps philosophical stories—and there are so many of them, so many more than one could admit when I first undertook to submit myself to that discipline—will appear both more unavoidable and less coherent to me than they had previously. They will be fragmented, it seems, into philosophemes and juxtaposed with nonphilosophy. They will be closed off by the horizon of the aphorism (the *horismos*), while opened up to language and history. In any case, this is what I read in Barthes's text, never intended for me, but appearing all the same in the mail.

Notes

1. Barthes, *Empire of Signs*, trans. Richard Howard (New York: Hill and Wang, 1982), p. 30.

2. References are to the numbered sections of Roland Barthes, *Camera Lucida: Reflections on Photography*, trans. Richard Howard (New York: Hill and Wang, 1981).

3. Hegel, *The Phenomenology of Spirit*, trans. A. V. Miller (Oxford: Clarendon Press, 1977), VIA; cf. also my essay "An Ancient Quarrel in Hegel's Phenomenology," *Owl of Minerva* (Spring 1986), 165–180.

4. Hegel, *The Phenomenology of Spirit*, p. 19.

5. Jacques Derrida, *Speech and Phenomena*, trans. David Allison (Evanston: Northwestern University Press, 1973), p. 54.

6. Friedrich Nietzsche, *Thus Spoke Zarathustra*, trans. Walter Kaufmann (New York: Penguin, 1978), p. 110.

7. Jacques Derrida, "Les morts de Roland Barthes," *Poétique* (September 1981), 269–292.

**RICHARD
HOWARD**

Remembering Roland Barthes

Mutual friends brought us together in 1957. He came to my door in the summer of that year, disconcerted by his classes at Middlebury (teaching students unaccustomed to a visitor with no English to speak of) and bearing, by way of introduction, a fresh-printed copy of *Mythologies*. (*Michelet* and *Writing Degree Zero* had already been published in France, but he was not yet known in America—not even in most French departments. Middlebury was enterprising.) Until his death in 1980, we remained intimates, and, as I continue translating his work (several books are still to be published here), the dialogue continues too, however lamely. He is a presence in my life, though one no longer to be addressed, a presence that speaks out of a silence, into a silence. Looking through two dozen letters, I find few items of literary interest— only the sort of thing an author tells a translator he knows pretty well: "You ask for the Hobbes references—mon petit Richard, perhaps I made them up! You must translate back into English and blame it on me in a footnote."

Now, of course, there are books, even in English, about his books. Indeed, what prompts reminiscence here is the introduction to *A Barthes Reader* (New York: Hill and Wang, 1984), one of Susan Sontag's finest essays and certainly the best single piece of writing I have seen about the figure, a word Barthes used when he meant more than a character, less than a person. I want to venture a couple of sketches of the person, whom I shall call—in order to differentiate my responses to him from those elicited by his texts—Roland. At Hannah Arendt's memorial service, I was struck by Mary McCarthy's observation that she did not want to discuss her friend's ideas "but to try to bring her back as a person, a physical being, showing herself radiantly in what she called the world of appearance, a stage from which she has now withdrawn." Something of the kind here, though Roland's radiance in that world was more reticent than Arendt's—a light *en veilleuse* (as a nightlight), as it were.

Whenever I went to Paris (though he was not always there: he would be in Dakar, in Italy, or in the family house in Hendaye and, returning to Paris, where he had been born and lived within four blocks all his life, would ask me about events in the city as if he were unfamiliar with Parisian diversions, Parisian prospects), I would take him a box of Havana cigars, which he relished extravagantly. He did not readily spend money on himself (though he liked being a host), and expensive cigars seemed a particularly American windfall, I guess. For all his sensitive texts about food— the pages on Japanese meals in *The Empire of Signs* seem to me the best French gastrotexts, as he might say, since Brillat-Savarin— Roland rarely joined me in restaurants. Not only did he live with his mother, he ate almost always at home. Dinners in the rue Servandoni (perhaps half a dozen come to mind) were simple yet festive, for Madame Barthes had the gift of not fussing, in what New Yorkers would call a fifth-floor walk-up. Even the dog, Lux, forbore. The tone in that family (there was a half-brother as well) was invariably affectionate, amiable to outsiders and charged with the sense that what was being withheld would be extended on further occasions.

Indeed, when Madame Barthes came to New York, in the middle 1960s—her first visit since 1904 and her first air travel!— more was offered: I joined them on the helicopter from the newly named Kennedy Airport, landing on top of the glittering heart of a city Madame Barthes could never have imagined from her first encounter with it, and from then on it was all pleasure. She immediately participated in her son's delight in the city, and one saw from her traveling costume where Roland got his taste for tweeds, and, after many visits to "Aber-Crombie," his love of a certain kind of "British" tailoring. And one saw from their way of being together, from an interest in each other quite without inquisitiveness, that this mother and this son were able—rarest of family rituals—to enjoy the world they shared. It was not necessarily his world (or hers), but that did not taint the sharing. My discovery that his mother did not read his books, and that Roland did not expect her to, eased some family tensions of my own; this was but one of many lessons my friend was to impart.

Roland was, as I suggest, a vigorous traveler though an inert conversationalist. In 1958 or 1959 we went to Amsterdam together, driving up from Paris through the February fogs that reduced (or extended) the auto routes into the Flemish landscapes he wrote about so splendidly. In the city, I recall my own astonishment at the lack of an immediate Eros in the faces and bodies we encountered, and I can still hear Roland's admonishment: "Mon petit Richard, don't you think there's a connection between the fact that the Dutch are the friendliest, most decent and civic-minded population in Europe and the fantasy that neither you nor I find them eroticized?" This was to be enlarged on in the essay on Pierre Loti, but the germ was there in the gay bars of Amsterdam. We went, on Roland's insistence, to Haarlem to visit the Franz Hals museum—though once in the presence of those five sinister ladies, "The Wives of the Regents," he would not speak, merely making sure I took in that infernal company. Walking along the canals afterward, I recall his saying that if his government became severely repressive (those were FLN days), he would move here, as French intellectuals since Voltaire had done; it was a preconceived exile he happened to be spared, but not one that he dreaded.

In New York, *le shopping*, mostly for clothes, became a considerable pastime, and concerts more than that. Italian opera was something of a fetish, though by 1969 Roland had given up the theater—I could not persuade him to go with me to any play in Paris. His years of writing for *Théâtre populaire* and the unsuccessful struggle to attach Brecht's ideas to the Parisian scene had discouraged him past the effort: "Not Claudel! Richard, in a Claudel play there's always an adultery and an altar, the one leads infallibly to the other." Music sustained him, however; after Sanford Friedman and I had given a big party for him (which I fear he hated), I remember asking what he'd like to do: "Just play your record of the slow movement of the Schubert trio Opus 99," he sighed, and lit a cigar. But it is not an anthology of Roland's tastes I would compile—rather, the *Stimmung*, the mood of detachment-cum-euphoria which was their goal: that's what I need to articulate. When I say Roland was inert in conversation, I mean that he felt enough at ease to let the silences hover and accumulate. I think he was thinking.

Sleep, for this man of vehement somnolences, was—a nightmare. During his last visit, when he spoke on Proust at the New York University Humanities Institute and hinted that he was writing a novel, or wanted to write one, I moved out of my apartment and turned it over to him. The place was transformed in two days: the blinds were never thick enough, nor the walls, and I suspect even the electric blanket failed to conform to his rigorous exigencies. This was Roland-as-Twentieth-Century-Man, with insomnia as the tragic muse: he confronted her with cigars, a little Campari, and, judging by the books left behind, Bataille and Sartre.

"I can do everything with my language, but not with my body. What I hide by my language my body utters. I can deliberately mold my message, not my voice. My body is a stubborn child, my language is a very civilized adult" (*A Lover's Discourse*, p. 45). Indeed, Roland's books were to become increasingly what Goethe had said his were: fragments of a great confession, or, as Sontag observes, a return to Montaigne. To his graceful, searching anatomy of himself, I can add only two notes: Roland's hands had the much reticulated palms of a very old monkey. They seemed to belong to another species, not to a man who wrote only with a fountain pen (I have never seen a typescript). His voice was resonant and what the French call *chantante:* he had studied singing with Charles Panzéra, and if we did not talk much about books ("You know what I liked so much about Japan? No one even thought of giving me a book!"), there was always Fauré . . .

I believe Roland hated his body, and I know he was perpetually at grips with his weight ("Oui, j'ai beaucoup engraissé, il

faut changer tout cela"), but there was none of the usual conflict—usual in my own experience, among intellectuals and in
myself—between vanity (the world) and narcissism (the self). He
was faithful to what Walter Pater, whom he had never heard of,
calls the administration of the visible; he adored the physical
world: "Desire still irrigates the non-will-to-possess by this per-
ilous movement: I love you in my head, but I imprison it behind
my lips. I do not divulge. I say silently to who is not yet or is
no longer the other: I keep myself from loving you" (*A Lover's
Discourse*).

The accents are those of Socrates, the first—as Roland was
the latest—Docent of Desire. I have never had a friend whose
affection exacted so little, and the rewards of our intimacy—beyond the pleasure of his texts—are beyond mourning, though the
loss is still felt. In the last letter, four months before he was run
down by that laundry truck, he wrote, "Don't think me indifferent
or ungrateful—it's just that since Maman's death there has been a
scission in my life, in my psyche, and I have less courage to un-
dertake things. Don't hold it against me. *Ne m'en veuillez pas.*"

MARY LYDON
with
LORI
WOODRUFF
AND SUSAN
WARREN

In Memoriam Roland Barthes

The Contract: A Stele for Roland Barthes

On écrit pour être aimé, on est lu sans pouvoir l'être, c'est sans doute cette distance qui constitue l'écrivain. (One writes to be loved, one is read without being able to be loved [read]. It is doubtless this distance that makes the writer.)
—Barthes

In Curtin Hall 209 on the morning of March 27, 1980, Jeanette Mische, a student at the University of Wisconsin–Milwaukee living in West Allis, raised her hand to ask if I knew that Roland Barthes had died. "I was getting ready for school," she said, "when my husband called from the next room, 'Do you know a French writer by the name of Roland Barthes?' 'Yes,' I answered, 'What about him?' 'He's dead.' I rushed in and grabbed the *Sentinel* out of his hand. He couldn't understand why I was so upset."

In Bolton Hall 170 that afternoon, according to an arrangement made the week before, two students, Lori Woodruff and Susan Warren, staged a performance piece. The class had just finished reading *Image—Music—Text* and the piece had been inspired by Barthes. Its point of departure was one section of the essay "Writers, Intellectuals, Teachers," which is called "The Contract," specifically the epigraph to that section, which reads as follows:

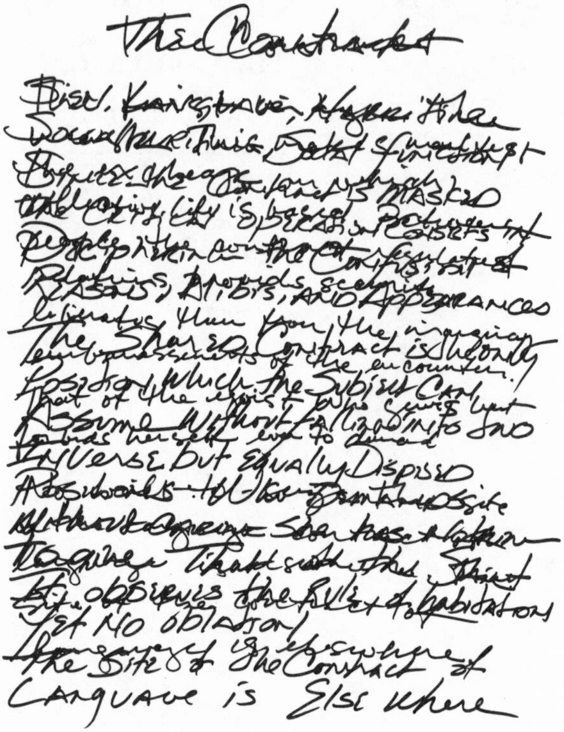

The Contract

[handwritten text, largely illegible] ... MASKED the City is ... in ... People ... Places, Alibis, and Appearances ... The Shared Contract is the only position which the Subject can resume without falling into two ... Inverse but Equally Disposed ... Such has ... require that ... observes the ... yet no obligation ... The Site of the Contract of Language is Elsewhere

THE CONTRACT	THE CONTRACT
THE FIRST IMAGE	SIGN, LANGUAGE, NARRATIVE, SOCIAL WRITING, SOCIAL FUNCTION
THE MASK	
THIS MAKES MANIFEST THE EXCHANGE ON WHICH COLLECTIVE LIFE IS BASED	SINCE THE CONTRACT IS MASKED, THE CRITICAL OPERATION CONSISTS IN DECIPHERING THE CONFUSION OF REASONS, ALIBIS, AND APPEARANCES
BETWEEN PEOPLE THE CONTRACT REGULATES RELATIONS, PROVIDES SECURITY, LIBERATES THEM FROM THE IMAGINARY EMBARRASSMENTS OF THE ENCOUNTER	

(WHAT AM I TO COUNT ON IN THE OTHER'S DESIRE?)
(WHAT AM I FOR HER?)

	THE SHARED CONTRACT IS THE ONLY POSITION WHICH THE SUBJECT CAN ASSUME WITHOUT FALLING INTO TWO INVERSE BUT EQUALLY DESPISED POSITIONS
THAT OF THE EGOIST	WHO DEMANDS WITHOUT CARING THAT SHE HAS NOTHING TO GIVE
	THAT OF THE SAINT
WHO GIVES BUT FORBIDS HERSELF EVER TO DEMAND	IT OBSERVES THE RULE OF HABITATION
NO WILL-TO-SEIZE	YET NO OBLIGATION
THE SITE OF THE CONTRACT OF LANGUAGE IS ELSEWHERE	THE SITE OF THE CONTRACT OF LANGUAGE IS ELSEWHERE

Most of the time, the relations between humans suffer,
often to the point of destruction, from the fact that the
contract established in those relations is not respected. As
soon as two human beings enter into reciprocal relationship, their contract, generally tacit, comes into force, regu-
lating the form of their relations, etc.'

—Brecht (*IMT*, p. 196)

The props for the piece consisted of a freestanding wooden
frame into which a sheet of glass measuring about three feet by
four feet was inserted. Lori and Susan, each armed with a crayon
(one red, one blue), positioned themselves on opposite sides of the
glass, face to face. This is their description of the performance
which followed and its residue: "In turns, we spoke the text of the
contract and then wrote our speech on the glass in colored crayon.
We recited the text once, exchanged places, then re-spoke and re-
wrote our contract. When we had finished, the glass was covered
with the marks of our writing, which was many-layered and therefore indecipherable."

By the end of the performance, the glass, once transparent,
an invisible barrier, had acquired a kind of discontinuous opacity.
Consequently, the view the writers had of each other had become
progressively obscured by their own production, their writing.
This development, so rich in implication not only for "relations
between humans," but for the uses of writing as well, recalls a
fragment from *Roland Barthes*, "La seiche et son encre—The cuttlefish and its ink," especially the opening sentence, "I am writing
this day after day; it takes, it sets: the cuttlefish produces its ink: I
tie up my image-system (in order to protect myself and at the
same time to offer myself)" (*RB*, p. 162).

But it was not only on the glass that the performance left its
trace. The audience, that other writing surface, equally palimp-
sestuous, registered certain impressions too; for instance, the
timbre of the performers' voices alternating with the clack of the
crayons on the glass, the rapid sweeping movement of hand and
arm in the gesture of writing (a gesture that was gradually seen to
engage the whole body, as the approach of the lower end of the
tablet obliged the writers to bend more and more to their work),
the cold bright light of the March sun streaming through the

classroom window, catching the blue and red marks on the glossy surface, illuminating the manuscript.

For the terms of the contract, see the photograph and its text.

As the last word, itself so poignant, so charged with nostalgia, died away, echoed by the staccato rat-a-tat of its inscription, my eyes filled. I was moved not only because Lori and Susan were young and clever and lovely and my students (though that were enough for tears) but also because "as chance would have it (but what is chance?)" (*S/Z*, p. 18) they had produced a stele for Roland Barthes. There it stood, glittering in the sunlight in the middle of Bolton 170, perfectly timed and executed, the spectral presence of "writing aloud," reverberating with the "grain of the voice" (*The Pleasure of the Text*, p. 66); not only *graphie* (the signifier without the signified) although spectacularly and uncannily that, but *écriture*, "scripture" being no longer available to us. Richard Klein has wickedly coined *écritoor*, but the rendering "personal utterance" is near enough. Barthes himself called it "the morality of form" (*Writing Degree Zero*, p. 15), which I take to mean that vital interplay between "writing" and "the relations between humans" which characterizes all his own work, which is indeed his subject, to which he constantly returns.

I believe that Barthes, who relished being photographed among his students, for whom the seminar was a space filled with "'the tangle of amorous relations'" (*RB*, p. 171), would have liked his stele: the finished form certainly, so uncannily like something out of his own image-repertoire, but more especially perhaps its production. Had he not, after all, defined meaning as

> any kind of intertextual or extratextual correlation, that is, every feature of the narrative which refers to another moment within it or to another locus of the culture required in order to read it. . . . Meaning for me (that is the way I live it in my research) is essentially a *quotation*, it is the point of departure of a code, that which allows us to set out in the direction of a code and what a code implies, even if the code has not been reconstructed or cannot be reconstructed. (*Exégèse et herméneutique*, pp. 185–86)

In other words, the name Roland Barthes led to no code for Jeanette's husband. It was for him, in effect, unreadable. This was not the case for Jeanette. For her "Roland Barthes" was a quotation: she had read it before. So too, for readers of Barthes, the text of Lori and Susan's contract was a constellation of codes (Barthes speaks throughout *S/Z* of the "starred" text, in which the orbit of meaning is plotted), codes for which words such as "oblation," "will-to-seize," "alibis" are all points of departure.

Readability, the conditions of readability, was Barthes's central concern. Reading is a "labor of language" and to read, for him,

> is to find meanings, and to find meanings is to name them;
> but these named meanings are swept towards other
> names; names call to each other, reassemble, and their
> grouping calls for further naming: I name, I unname, I
> rename: so the text passes: it is a nomination in the course
> of becoming, a tireless approximation, a metonymic labor.
> (*S/Z*, p. 11)

So too the world passes, the world which is for Barthes a vast text; hence reading is not and must not be limited to the printed word. Women's clothes, margarine, soap powders, plastic, striptease are also signs or sign systems to be read. Reading therefore is seen to be a vital activity, passionate and political.

But so too life passes. The reading subject, "This 'I' which approaches the text," in Barthes's words "is already itself a plurality of other texts, of codes which are infinite or, more precisely, lost (whose origin is lost)" (*S/Z*, p. 10). Thus, reading is always rereading, recognition, in the same way that Freud tells us finding is always finding again. It is no wonder then that Barthes favors the word "text," insisting on its etymology, its derivation from the Latin *textus*, tissue, suggesting weaving or braiding, as in the word "textile." It is the play in the word "text" that allows Barthes to produce one of the most illuminating and thrilling descriptions of reading and its complement, writing, that have ever been given:

> The text while it is being produced is like a piece of Valen-
> ciennes lace created before us under the lacemaker's fin-
> gers: each sequence undertaken hangs like the tempo-
> rarily inactive bobbin waiting while its neighbour works;
> then, when its turn comes, the hand takes up the thread
> again, brings it back to the frame; and as the pattern is

filled out, the progress of each thread is marked with a
pin which holds it and is gradually moved forward: thus
the terms of the sequence: they are positions held and
then left behind in the course of a gradual invasion of
meaning. This process is valid for the entire text. The
grouping of codes, as they enter into the work, into the
movement of the reading, constitutes a braid (*text, fabric,
braid:* the same thing); each thread, each code, is a voice;
these braided—or braiding—voices from the writing:
when it is alone, the voice does not labor, transforms
nothing: it *expresses;* but as soon as the hand intervenes
to gather and intertwine the inert threads, there is labor,
there is transformation. We know the symbolism of the
braid: Freud, considering the origin of weaving, saw it as
the labor of a woman braiding her pubic hairs to form the
absent penis. The text, in short, is a fetish; and to reduce
it to the unity of meaning, by a deceptively univocal reading, is to *cut the braid,* to sketch the castrating gesture.
(*S/Z,* p. 160)

What "nomination in the process of becoming" is involved in
the production of that very text itself! The reader-producer, if she
is truly to read, must pass from Valenciennes lace (Vermeer's portrait of the lacemaker, bent over her pillow) to Freud (psychoanalysis—humbug or genial discovery, depending on the codes
which constitute the reading "I"—his essay on femininity, for the
"I" which recognizes weaving as the departure of a code) to fetish
(the absent penis of the mother, that which is present and absent
at once, if the code is Freud, object of unwarranted veneration if it
is le Président de Brosses: *Le culte des dieux fétiches,* 1760).

The text as fetish is probably still one of Barthes's most scandalous pronouncements, at least for Anglo-Saxon readers; yet
which of us, student or teacher, has not asked ourselves, "What to
write now? Can you still write anything?" (*RB,* p. 188). The text,
whether term paper or magnum opus, is always woven over an
absence. "One writes with one's desire" (*RB,* p. 188), and where
nothing is lacking, nothing is desired. How much of writing is intended to hide the scandalous fact that we have nothing to say?
Like the cuttlefish, we eject our ink and dart away under its cover:
writing as alibi, "The site of the contract of language is elsewhere."

And if we may have nothing to say, then how to begin? Barthes writes appreciatively of the rules established by classical rhetoric to facilitate beginnings: "In my opinion," he writes, "these rules are related to a feeling that there is an aphasia native to man, that it is difficult to speak, that there is perhaps nothing to say, and that it is necessary, therefore, to have a whole set of rules, a protocol, in order to find out *what* to say: *invenire quid dicas*" (*EH*, p. 192).

Language is an infinite structure; how therefore justify beginning here rather than anywhere else? The anxiety attendant on beginnings is clearly related to the castrating gesture. One must "cut in," but at precisely the right point, and as it were, on the bias, lest the whole fabric (braid) come away in the hand, the threads (hairs) inactive, dead.

It is curious that there is one book in Barthes's corpus which is rarely commented upon (it is one of the two which have not been translated into English). I refer to his book on Michelet, number 19 in the series of which *Roland Barthes* is number 96. The format of this series is quite strictly homogeneous: the first image is always the subject's handwriting, the second his portrait. This is the order followed in Barthes's *Michelet*, but in *Roland Barthes* the portrait of the artist is supplanted by a photo of his mother, clad in a full-skirted dress. The last image in the book is an anatomist's sketch of the human body, showing only the veins and arteries; the effect is of a shaggy anthropoid. The accompanying text reads as follows:

> To write the body.
> Neither the skin, nor the muscles, nor the bones,
> nor the nerves, but the rest: an awkward, fibrous,
> shaggy, raveled thing, a clown's coat

The final words of the text, written in white on the black surface of the inner back cover, are, "I am not through desiring." From the mother's skirts to the clown's coat, so passes Roland Barthes's text: a trajectory of desire, as all texts are, a quest for the object irremediably lost, the mother. Born naked into the world, we must write our garment, leap into language, weave our text. Barthes, by articulating his own metonymic process, his own text, provides us with a new rhetoric, a new code of rules, a safety net.

The consequences of Barthes's work for practice, both pedagogic and critical, are therefore enormous. He chose for his adversary Doxa, received opinion, "what goes without saying," the tacit tyranny of ideology. His goal, like Freud's, was articulation: speech, writing, movement. The contract whether social, personal, or pedagogic must be articulated, then labored over and transformed.

The epigraph to the book on Michelet is one of Michelet's own sayings: "I am a complete man possessing the two sexes of the mind." Let it stand as epitaph for the man who could read it in Michelet's text, for whom it was a quotation, the departure of a code, Roland Barthes.

From the

Linguistic to

the Literary

JEAN-JACQUES
THOMAS

System vs. Code: A Semiologist's Etymology

Are not the human sciences etymological in pursuit of the etymon (origin and truth) of each phenomenon?
        —*Roland Barthes by Roland Barthes* (1975)

Readers of Barthes's work cannot fail to remark that *The Fashion System*, published in 1967, three years after *Elements of Semiology*, contains the word "system" in its title and that the book itself is divided into two parts: "The Vestimentary Code" and "The Rhetorical System." Its conclusion is entitled "Economy of the System." *S/Z*, published in 1970, starts with a presentation of the five codes which are used to read the novella by Balzac. In *A Theory of Semiotics*, Umberto Eco writes:

> Only this complex form of rule may properly be called a "code." Nevertheless, in many contexts the term [code] covers not only the phenomenon (d) (as in the case of the Morse code) but also the notion of purely combinational systems such as (a), (b), (c). For instance, the so-called "phonological code" is a system like (a); the so-called "genetic code" seems to be a system like (c); the so-called code of "kinship" is either an underlying com-

binational system like (a) or a system of pertinent parent-
hood units very similar to (b).[1]

What (a), (b), or (c) designates here is less important than the
fact that any system can be assimilated to a code of one sort or
another. That explains why, in the rest of his book, Eco eliminates
the term "system" and relies exclusively on the general notion of
code. Chapter 3 is simply entitled "Theory of Codes." Does this
mean that, in the late 1970s, the term "system" has lost its theoretical value, especially in the field of semiotics associated with
literary criticism? In fact, Eco's simple assimilation of the two
is misleading and it is with confidence that we can go back to
what he calls "the empirical roots of the homonymy" to consider
why, in recent European practice of semiology and specifically in
Barthes's corpus, the opposition between the two terms has been
created, cultivated, and maintained.

While Eco and most of the English-speaking semioticians
elide any functional difference between "code" and "system,"
Barthes sees an important distinction between the two and does
not use them indifferently (what Eco calls their "homonymy"). It is
my contention that the opposition between code and system found
in Barthes's early works is intellectual as well as functional and
that the former is deeply rooted in the history of both European
formalism and continental structuralism. It is also remarkable
that when Barthes abandons formal-descriptive structuralist practice after *The Pleasure of the Text* (1973), the intellectual distinction
explicitly manifested by the two words remains productive.

The 1916 publication of Saussure's *Course of General Linguistics* and the formalist writings of the Prague and Moscow
School inspired by the *Course* both aspire to scientific status.
In this sense, they set their studies of language apart from the
impressionistic or sociological traditions that preceded them.
Barthes's writings do not, at first, hide their affiliation with the
body of formalist works. It should also be mentioned that, in the
early 1950s, A. J. Greimas received a large grant to form a research group whose purpose was to produce a typology of traditional ethnic garments and that many future literary critics influenced by Russian formalism—Barthes and Michael Riffaterre
among them—were closely associated with this project. It is now
well established that Barthes's reading of P. Bogatyrev's "Func-

tion of Garment in Moravian Slovenia" during this period directed his interest toward a functional study of clothing's evolution. Three little-known articles hidden from Barthes's "official" bibliography clearly indicate this early interest in a taxonomy of garments and the evolution of clothing: "Histoire et sociologie du vêtement" (History and Sociology of Clothing, 1957), "Tricots à domicile" (Knitting at Home, 1959) and "Langage et vêtement" (Language and Clothing, 1959). Eventually, the notes and 3×5 cards written during this period resulted in the applied study known as *The Fashion System*.

These related projects led Barthes to organize the categories and operational concepts in the form of a manual that first appeared in 1964 under the title *Elements of Semiology*. As Louis-Jean Calvet recognizes, Barthes's title mirrors the most celebrated linguistic manual of the time: André Martinet's 1960 *Elements of General Linguistics* (2nd ed., Paris: Armand Colin, 1961).[2] For Barthes, the period is one of more or less complete adherence to the "monster of scientific totality." There is little doubt that at least the first part of *Elements* is based on the polar oppositions of function found in the *Course* and that the second part seeks to adapt the system of oppositions proposed by Trubetzkoy in order to define phonological peculiarities in terms of operative oppositions that are bilateral, proportional, and privative. It is Barthes's respect for the scientific dimension of linguistics that explains and justifies the reversal of priorities that he proposes when he writes: "In fact, we must now face the possibility of inverting Saussure's declaration: linguistics is not a part of the general science of signs, even a privileged part, it is semiology which is a part of linguistics."[3]

Many critics have interpreted this statement as a radical gesture by Barthes to move away from orthodox structuralism. I see quite the contrary. At a moment when he wanted to establish a rigorous semiology based on the Saussurean model, Barthes needed to protect the enterprise by covering it with the authority borrowed from the established discipline of linguistics: "The *Elements* here presented have as their sole aim the extraction from linguistics of analytical concepts which we think *a priori* to be sufficiently general to start semiological research on its way" (*Elements*, p. 12). Within this general context of intellectual affiliations, personal clinamen, and theoretical influence, the distinction between code and system which runs throughout *Elements* is the only one which will survive once Barthes disregards direct use of the taxonomic categories and the terminology established during the structuralist period.

But what is the difference between code and system and what does it cover? In *Elements*, the concept of code is discussed specifically in paragraphs I.1.6 ("Some Problems"), I.2.5 ("Complex Systems"), and III.3.5 ("Binarism") and is usually considered in relation with the notion of message. Starting with "I.2.2: The Garment System," the concept of system appears frequently and even in the main title of part III, "Syntagm and System." First it should be said that Barthes did not borrow the polar opposition between code and system directly from the *Course* as he did for the couplings of "Language/Speech," "Signified/Signifier," "Denotation/Connotation," and—less directly—"Syntagm/System." The term "code" does not appear in Saussure's *Course;* yet the term "system," endowed with a polemical value, is clearly a key word in it. In the first pages of the "Introduction," the term "system" is opposed to "history." When one studies language, one must distinguish between the *system* of the language and its *history.* The term "system" takes on the meaning of "synchronic structure" and thus emblematizes the opposition with the then traditional view of the linguistic establishment according to which the task at hand, for linguistics, was to look at language as a domain marked by a diachronic (historical) evolution. The second appearance of the term "system" occurs in a chapter devoted to the nature of the sign. There it takes a slightly different meaning: "Language is a system, and because of that it is not arbitrary and it is governed by a relative order." Now we are closer to the notion of code since the notion of system refers to the notion of language, the term designating the internal conventions controlling any tongue.

Since the source of the distinction between code and system cannot be found in the *Course* and will not be found in the work of the formalists, it is fair to say that the opposition proposed by Barthes constitutes an original contribution. This is the case not only for the structuralist terminology, but also for the diversification of the operative concepts which form the structuralist model. In fact, in this ensemble composed mostly from bits and pieces borrowed directly from other texts, the distinction proposed by Barthes helped him to homogenize and articulate within a unified view of semiology materials coming from Saussure and the Russian formalists which are sometimes seen as antagonistic. The character of personal contribution may also explain why, even after Barthes seemingly renounces his structuralist origins, he remains faithful to the implicit distinction of his invention.

For Barthes, the notion of system is close to the paradigmatic axis (the linguistic associative process) while code is closer to a syntagmatical concatenation (the linguistic combinational process). This analogy is confirmed in *Elements* by the fact that, in chapter III, Barthes himself opposes syntagm to system by basing his opposition on an elementary dichotomy inherited from Saussure: "For Saussure, the relationships between linguistic terms can develop on two planes, each of which generates its own particular values; these two planes correspond to two forms of mental activity. . . . The first plane is that of the *syntagms;* the syntagm is a combination of signs, which has space as a support. . . . The second plane is that of the associations (if we still keep Saussure's terminology)." Barthes pursues the distinction even further by implying that it also has relevance for the distinction between language and speech, one of the four Saussurean distinctions: "The associative plane has evidently a very close connection with 'language' as system, while the syntagm is nearer to speech. It is possible to use a subsidiary terminology: syntagmatic connections are *relations* in Hjelmslev, *continuities* in Jakobson, *contrasts* in Martinet; systematic relations are *correlations* in Hjelmslev, *similarities* in Jakobson, *oppositions* in Martinet."

Furthermore, following Jakobson's categories, this distinction also has direct implications for differentiating between metaphor and metonymy, the two main types of figurative discourse: "Saussure had an intimation that the syntagmatic and the associative (that is, for us, the systematic) probably corresponded to two forms of mental activity, which meant an excursion outside linguistics. Jakobson has adopted this extension by applying the opposition of the metaphor (of the systematic order) and the metonymy (of the syntagmatic order) to non-linguistic languages" (my emphasis). Here again, one can see Barthes's insistence on paraphrasing Jakobson's terminology; or rather, on rephrasing in his own terms a fundamental distinction that is already well accepted. This reformulation does not simply spring from a desire to impose his own mark on the methodology. It is an operation of coining imposed upon Barthes by the fact that he is attempting a transfer of the operative concepts from linguistics to semiology. Since Barthes sees the distinction between code and system as cutting across already well-established linguistic categories, it is now necessary to consider how it helps him to enumerate, organize, and distribute the components of his revised semiology.

In *Elements*, Barthes says that what Saussure's *Course* calls *associative relationships* he will call *systematic relationships*. These, in turn, are marked by substitution: one word for another within a paradigmatic series. Although the term "systematic" is a theoretical neologism, Barthes nevertheless reverts to a methodological material coming from his recent research and marked by the formalist influence. The examples given have to do with clothing. Thus, pants, shorts, and kilts appear together within a "systematic" relation, while a syntagmatic relation unites shoes, pants, jacket, and hat. Once the principle is established, the task at hand is to define the combinatory rules. In this area, Barthes envisions a model pattern of combinations in three parts such as the glossematics proposed earlier by the Danish linguist Louis Hjelmslev: "The three types of relation which . . . two syntagmatic units can enter into when they are contiguous: (i) a relation of solidarity: when they necessarily imply each other; (ii) of simple implication, when one implies the other without reciprocity; (iii) of combination, when neither implies the other."

Continuing his analysis of the inner workings of a semiological structure, Barthes refers to Martinet's work on phonetics in order to explain the type of relations existing between the different elements of the associative field. This movement away from his own terminology forces him to be more explicit: "The internal arrangement of the terms in an associative or paradigmatic field is usually called—at least in linguistics, and more precisely, in phonology—an opposition." The term "phonology" used here suggests that Barthes is referring to the Prague School and more precisely to Trubetzkoy's seminal 1939 work, *Grundzüge der Phonologie.* But strangely enough, in a following passage, Barthes tries to obscure the direct link between the scheme of semiological oppositions he is proposing and their archaeology in the field of phonology:

> We know that since human language is doubly articulated, it comprises two sorts of oppositions: the *distinctive* oppositions (between phonemes), and the *significant* oppositions (between monemes). Trubetzkoy has suggested a classification of the distinctive oppositions, which J. Cantineau has tried to adopt and extend to the significant oppositions in the language (*Cahiers Ferdinand de Saussure*, IX [pp. 11–40]). . . . We shall give here Cantineau's classification, for even if it cannot be easily applied (subsequently) to the semiological oppositions, it has the advantage of bringing to our notice the main problems posed by the structure of oppositions. (*Elements*, p. 75; my emphasis)

By using a secondhand classification, Barthes builds his semiology on a strange linguistic syncretism which now needs to be sorted out. At the outset of his semiological work, Barthes writes: "It would be advisable henceforth to adopt the distinction suggested by A. J. Greimas: *semantic* = referring to the content; *semiological* = referring to the expression" (*Elements*, p. 45, n. 41). From this distinction, he suggests the notion of semiological signifieds (the meaning of signifiers), leaving outside of his field of analysis the signified. It is important to note that Trubetzkoy's study of phonological oppositions had already done this. Studying the functions of the phonemes, Trubetzkoy proposes a schema which clearly (by nature) leaves semantics out and shows that his only real interest lies in the study of the signifiers. Also, at the level of the phonetic component of the signifier, Trubetzkoy creates a major distinction between two types of opposition: *phonological* and *distinctive*. For him, the phonological opposition deals with phonic distinctions only (vocalic, consonantic, and prosodic peculiarities of the phonemes), while the distinctive opposition leads to stylistic values and eventually to phonological signifieds. Obviously, the distinctive opposition in the Trubetzkoy terminology is close, *mutatis mutandis*, to what Barthes calls "significant opposition" and opposed to what he calls "distinctive opposition." It is also perfectly clear if one compares the notion of "significant oppositions" advanced by Barthes in *Elements of Semiology* to that of "distinctive oppositions" proposed by

Trubetzkoy in *Grundzüge der Phonologie:* namely, that it is one and the same taxonomy ("bilateral," "multilateral," "proportional," "privative," "equipollent," "constant," and "neutralized").

Of course, Barthes does not present these categories as his own. But at least he adopts them and introduces his own comments to support this taxonomy; nor does he hide that he found the title of his 1953 book, *Writing Degree Zero,* while studying the problems surrounding the notion of privative opposition. How, then, is it possible that, despite the same terminology, Barthes would reject the preexisting category of "distinctive opposition" advanced by Trubetzkoy and would instead propose the new category of significant opposition, which has no historical precedent, while transferring under this new label all the types of oppositions found in the original category proposed by Trubetzkoy? It is difficult to believe that the work of Cantineau (rather unknown and of little influence within linguistics) would authorize and justify the outright rejection of the overwhelming authority of Trubetzkoy. Here again, the missing link seems to be the eponymic text by Martinet. In this general discussion concerning oppositions, Martinet is mentioned in passing and on a rather minor point. But it is clear that, in *Elements of General Linguistics,* Martinet builds an impressive analytic apparatus on the elementary differentiation between distinctive oppositions and significant oppositions. In fact, this dichotomy serves as the basis for Martinet's concept of double articulation, a concept which is far from unchallenged since it is only one of the many possible extrapolations from the work of Trubetzkoy and other linguists from the Prague School. (In fact, the so-called generative phonology of the 1970s openly challenges Martinet's view.)

Barthes's seemingly neutral and ecumenical statement concerning the classification of oppositions—"We know that since human language is doubly articulated, it comprises"—can thus be rewritten as "following Martinet, we can accept the idea that human language is doubly articulated." (In fact, Barthes has already used the concept of the double articulation twice: in sections II.1.2 and III.2.4.) But, in both instances, he has presented it as Martinet's. The latter instance is remarkable in that the concept is treated as accepted and indisputable. Barthes has created an authoritative truth (*naturel-qui-va-de-soi*) on the order of an axiom, one of the false evidences that he had so vigorously denounced in *Mythologies*. Nevertheless, the result of this assimilation of conflicting influences leads Barthes to define his notion of "system" as a substitute for that of "paradigm" with one major difference: whereas a paradigm is merely perceived as a collection of commutable units, Barthes functionalizes the ensemble and emphasizes the relationship between units by introducing into the collection the potentiality of internal oppositional dynamics borrowed from phonology.

After designating the canonical texts which compose the many layers upon which Barthes builds his dynamic and operative concept of system, let us turn now toward his concept of code, which, as I indicated at the beginning of this essay, offers less clear traces of past influences. In the first chapter, the preliminary discussion of the difference between language (*langue*) and speech (*parole*)—which nowadays would undoubtedly emphasize the notion of code—does not display the term. The term "code" does appear in a nonattributed quote "speech: . . . is made in the first place of the combination thanks to which the speaking subject can use the code of the language with a view to expressing his personal thought" (*Elements*, p. 15). This is not a direct quote from Saussure's *Course*. The first explicit use of the term by Barthes occurs in an unmarked context where it seemingly needs no further explanation: "Is it possible to identify the language with the code and the speech with the message?" (*Elements*, p. 18).

Clearly, the clinamen of influence has played its role here since, in the earlier discussion of the difference between language and speech, Barthes had defined language as "a system of contractual values" (*Elements*, p. 14). The homonymy manifested here between the terms "code" and "system" is probably the result of the fact that the whole passage is a simple reformulation of the ideas expressed in the *Course*. The terms "system" and "code" can be understood as denoting the same organization of minimal units; neither has been given a technical (idiolectic) meaning by Barthes. Not surprisingly, the linguists Barthes invokes in relation to the definition of code are his contemporaries André Martinet and Pierre Guiraud. A second use of the term "code" is more specific: "the rolled *r* . . . in the speech of the theater, for instance . . . signals a country accent and therefore is a part of a code, without which the message of 'ruralness' could not be either emitted or perceived" (*Elements*, p. 20). Here the term indicates that Barthes is still referring to an organization of minimal units but that this organization *per se* has gained a certain significative value. The grouping of certain elements as a system is not only functional; it also conveys a certain signification that explains the notion of "message" in the sentence quoted above.

Barthes's terminology undergoes a final slippage in I.1.8 ("Duplex Structures"), where the term "message"—used casually to denote that which carries a signification in the last passage quoted above—is elevated to the status of specialized term in an implied analogy between *language/speech* and *code/message*. First, one can see that Barthes has rejected the objections of Hjelmslev and Guiraud in order to follow Martinet in thinking that the chiasmatic identification of language with code and speech with message is possible. But, more importantly for my analysis, one can see that system has been eliminated from the definition of language (*langue*) in favor of code. To be sure, the latter term acquires a specific technical value briefly exploited in the subsequent analysis of Jakobson's theory of the "duplex structures."

In subsequent works, Barthes clearly understands the notion of semiological code as the process of linking certain elements within an ensemble which would carry a message of its own. This definition is not explicitly expressed in *Elements of Semiology*, but in II.3.2 ("Classification of the Signifiers"), where he anticipates that one of the two operations of structuration will consist in "classify(ing) the syntagmatic relations which link these (linguistic) units" while, as we have seen, the system takes care of the regrouping of these units into dynamic "paradigmatic classes." This understanding of the notion of code explains why Barthes can elevate any concept, notion, or word to the status of an emblematic term which will serve as the catalyst for the code and as its label. A code, therefore, is a semiological ensemble which is empirically defined and open. For example, *S/Z* determines the five codes as imposed by the specific reading of the text. Barthes always maintains that another reader could have found different codes and would probably not have selected the same number. It is therefore ironic to discover subsequent studies of literary texts that claim to follow Barthes by simply transposing the five codes onto another text. In so doing, they practice exactly what Barthes has denounced, explaining that this type of approach simply destroys the difference between texts (*S/Z*, p. 10). A code is always the product of an immanent determinism unique to the specific text itself and each text generates its own codes.

During the neoformalist era of the 1960s and early 1970s, Michael Riffaterre and Tzvetan Todorov also elevated the notion of code to the rank of operative concept. Even within this context, Barthes's understanding of the nature of a code remains original. For Riffaterre, the network of codes in a literary text is empirically defined but closed. There is a finite and necessary number of codes recognized by every reader through a hermeneutical reading. The reader is bound eventually to uncover the necessary codes hidden in the text and cannot create his or her own set of codes independently from intratextual determinism. For Todorov, codes are logically defined: both closed and transtextual. They preexist any text and form a grid that a critic can transfer from text to text in order to evaluate the conformity of any single text to a standard pattern. This is the case, for example, for the codes defined in *The Fantastic: An Introduction* (1970). Either they are present in a text that can be said to belong to the fantastic genre or they are not and the text falls outside the scope of fantastic literature.

The syntagmatic nature of the Barthes code allows him to place in the same code objects which come from different and sometimes antithetical paradigmatic series. Barthes submits to the imperative of structure, but the choice of the objects and the nature of the structure remains his own. This state of affairs gives him great ease in determining the elements and general shape of the code. But contrary to what happens to his definition of system, Barthes does not elaborate the nature of the relationships among the elements which compose the code, where the dynamics of differences among the elements involved in a gem were regulated according to the types of opposition. Among the three types of syntagmatic relation proposed by Hjelmslev, Barthes chooses the least binding and demanding: that of combination ("when neither [element] implies the other"). This lack of specific functional model for the code explains why Barthes progressively abandons the modeling of his codes to the "demon of analogy." From then on, in Barthes's essays, a code can become a subjective jumble of heterogeneous objects as long as they are perceived as associated by him. The writings which take the form of fragments can then be seen as collections of topics codified in a compact form. In *Roland Barthes by Roland Barthes*, for example, the entry "Migraines" reveals a code which encompasses (among others) objects such as social divisions, Michelet, childhood, city/countryside, work, phobia, body, theater, and symbolization.

The format of collected fragments in Barthes's later writings should allow for a clearer understanding of the conceptual slippage between system and code. In Barthes's own terminology, his first writings were marked by a conception of criticism as the elaboration of systems, while the second is characterized by the conception of criticism as *bricodage*, an invented portmanteau term combining the activities of secondary usage (*bricolage*) studied by Lévi-Strauss and an interest in reconfiguring fragments into personalized codes that Barthes explores increasingly. The turning point for Barthes is *S/Z*. What is extraordinary is the fact that, historically, this text brings to the fore the notion of code as a possible critical tool while the title emblematizes and emphasizes the typical mark of opposition ("/") between two phonemes that is the operative concept at the core of the system.

Barthes was fully conscious of the perils of analogy. In *Roland Barthes by Roland Barthes*, he writes, "All scientific explanations which resort to analogy . . . participate in the lure, they form the image-repertory of Science" (*Roland Barthes*, p. 44). One may then wonder whether Barthes was conscious of the fact that, by defining the operative concept of code and using it in a privileged way, he was in effect designating himself as a scientific outsider. In the entry entitled "Denotation as the Truth of Language," Barthes returns to the notion of etymon which gives this essay its title: "Denotation would here be a scientific myth: that of a 'true' state of language, as if every sentence had inside it an *etymon* (origin and truth). . . . Each time I believe in truth, I need denotation" (*Roland Barthes*, p. 67).

In order to measure the implicit importance of this passage so as to understand Barthes's own etymology, it is necessary to bring in an echoing text. In *The Postmodern Condition*, Jean-François Lyotard remarks that the appearance of the concept of modernity corresponds to that of scientific positivism at the end of the nineteenth century. For Lyotard, the principles governing scientific knowledge as defined by positivism are as follows: "Scientific knowledge demands that one stays away from playing with language: what is required is denotation. The only criterion of acceptability of an occurrence is its truth-value. . . . An occurrence should result in a denotation. One, therefore, knows (in a positivist way) only if one can produce a true utterance about a referent; and one is scientific only if one can produce verifiable utterances about referents accessible to experts."[4]

If the scientific basis of modernity is denotation, then Barthes's semiology, marked by a direct affiliation with scientific linguistics, should be founded on denotation and should result in conclusions which can be judged according to their truth-value within a well-defined system. Yet a study based upon codes as Barthes understands them—relying mostly on the whimsical choice of analogical, homological, and metonymical bridges—can only function in a truth-suspending mode. The value of the polysemic and plural meaning so acquired exceeds the accepted limit of denotation and offers itself to the infinite openness of collective interpretation, where its value is determined by the practices ruling the marketplace for such random commodities.

There can be little or no doubt that Barthes's early involvement with semiology was motivated by the ambition of defining a new scientific methodology. This is confirmed by the fact that in *Roland Barthes by Roland Barthes*, published after the shift visible in *S/Z* and *The Pleasure of the Text*, one of the few fragments devoted to science has to do with semiology in the unmistakable form of a fetish. In "Science Dramatized," Barthes does not dispute the fact that semiology once had a scientific status. He only accuses it of having lost its eagerness to go to the end of its scientific project:

> Thus, he thought, it was because it could not be carried
> away that semiological science had not turned out well: it
> was so often no more than a murmur of indifferent labors,
> each of which made no differentiation among object, text,
> body. Yet how could it be forgotten that semiology has
> some relation to the passion of meaning, its apocalypse
> and/or its utopia? (*Roland Barthes*, pp. 160–161)

But who (or what) lost eagerness? Barthes himself admits that he wants to ease himself out of formalism and concedes that this easing out is also the sign of combat fatigue ("the deliberate loss of all heroism") and of the search for intellectual comfort. The uphill fight for the etymon (the telos?) has to be abandoned. No more utopia, just the livable *atopia* organized on codes which process "invested and superficial" intellectual objects that pass and disappear as word-objects in a freewheeling discourse.

Lyotard and many philosophers of his generation believe that science and modernity belong to the same project of knowledge. It is then easy to interpret the statement (in *Roland Barthes by Roland Barthes*) of sudden indifference toward the modern as a radical indifference to the scientific project as well. The erasure of difference, present as an underlying leitmotif in all these quotes, signifies the magnitude of the crisis of scientific confidence lived by Barthes in the early 1970s. During the exultant period of his will-to-know (*vouloir-savoir* or *volonté de savoir*), Barthes wrote that science existed only through difference: science, sign, difference, system, and the hope of taking heroic risks to reach utopia! In later years, he was confined to the somber bureaucracy of the man of letters: commodities, objects, fragments, indifference and *codes*. Condemned to the dark side of scientific knowledge, the writer manipulates his 3×5 cards and lets his *oeuvre* grow by accretion, accepting the fact that it is no longer the repository of a forthcoming apocalypse.

Notes

1. Umberto Eco, *A Theory of Semiotics* (Bloomington: Indiana University Press, 1976), p. 37.

2. Calvet writes, "It can therefore be seen that the *Elements of Semiology* constitutes the most orthodox of Barthes's texts from the point of view of structural linguistics. In this will to scientificity that characterized it at the time, the author was obliged to proceed step by step and to adopt the very demeanor of linguists as it appeared to him on the basis of the *Elements of General Linguistics*" (*Roland Barthes: Regard politique sur le signe* [Paris: Payot, 1973], p. 37).

3. Barthes, *Elements of Semiology*, trans. Annette Lavers and Colin Smith (New York: Hill and Wang, 1968), p. 11.

4. Jean-François Lyotard, *The Postmodern Condition: A Report on Knowledge*, trans. Geoff Bennington and Brian Massumi (Minneapolis: University of Minnesota Press, 1984), p. 47.

ANTOINE
COMPAGNON

The Two Barthes

Translated by
James McGuire and Didier Bertrand

At various intervals over the last hundred years or more, perhaps even since 1800 and the publication of Mme de Staël's *De la lit-térature*, someone has been sounding the alarm: the relations between literary criticism and history are not what they should be. Shall I, in turn, sound the alarm?

Here are some of the distinguished Cassandras, my predecessors: in France, Hippolyte Taine, Gustave Lanson, Lucien Febvre, and Roland Barthes; in Germany, Walter Benjamin and Hans Robert Jauss; and some of the Russian formalists such as Jakobson and Tynianov. All to no avail.

We are coming out of a period when the theoretical approach to the literary text dominated. We are not even certain of having totally left it behind. There is, in fact, no reason to hope to leave it behind. There lingers, however, the definite feeling that an era (an episteme?) has come to an end: nothing new under the sun; theory is no longer in its prime; each one cultivates his own garden; the collective faith wilts.

The epoch—the great period—of literary theory broke the long and absolute domination of the historical treatment of literature, referred to as literary history since about 1900 and the apotheosis of Lansonism. Synchrony or diachrony, structure or history, according to the stiff unwieldy alternative, the old dilemma that Saussure, among others, revived at the beginning of the century. The time would have henceforth come for the pendulum to swing back.

But neither is it certain that literary theory—in its days of glory, a parenthesis—has truthfully (*truly??*) and profoundly shaken the institutional domination of literary history. The latter persisted undisturbed for the most part while, elsewhere, formalisms were built up under various names: structuralism, poetics, semiology, semiotics . . . Let's talk about the New Criticism as a whole.

Paradoxically—oddly at the very least—literary theory of the sixties and seventies—the so-called formal, systematic, hard approach—has been diluted with a more personal, subjective, almost intimist criticism, just as wine is diluted with water or water with wine. I do not say this to explain the permanence of literary history in spite of the New Criticism: the latter would have been indecisive, ambiguous, not knowing what it wanted other than setting itself in opposition. But it has often been emphasized (whether out of hostility or complicity) that there were, for example, two Barthes: the rough and the tender, the hedonist and the methodist. It is too easy to reply that one came after the other. Doesn't this division have something to do with the destiny of literary history and theory, the decline (if decline there is) of theory, the revival (if revival there is) of history?

Emerging ready to fight at the close of the Algerian War, the New Criticism stood up against literary history. There were a few open and bloody confrontations, like the quarrel between Raymond Picard and Roland Barthes after *Sur Racine*.[1] Besides these, it was mainly an exchange of head-on or backhanded blows to gain influence. And in the case I am mentioning, it was the champion of tradition who launched the attack. What I mean to say is this: it is not certain that literary theory sought out the controversy or that it considered—except for the fleeting circumstances of the polemic—its foundation against literary history (revolt does not necessarily imply reflection), either theoretically or historically. As if history and theory, in truth, had preferred to avoid each other. As if—even though they both dealt with literature, but what is literature if not an open house?—as if history and theory were two self-contained worlds, two universes with nothing in common. How, from that time on, could one conceive of their mutual animosity promoted to misunderstanding?

My hypothesis on the matter is that there was a blind spot, an omission on the part of the New Criticism concerning its relation to literary history. It is because of this omission, like a worm in the apple, that it languishes today—if we admit that it languishes. (It is easy to say that the New Criticism denied history. Why would it have reflected on its relation to history? Precisely so that this denial would not be just a petition of principle but a reasoned affirmation.)

Literary history, from the time (the Dreyfus case roughly) that it asserted itself as a progressivist and modernist discipline— for it was thus before becoming that scarecrow for avant-gardes— literary history was rebelling against a criticism that was considered the cream of the crop: Lemaitre and France, Brunetière and Faguet. This "old old criticism" was accused by the new history of either dogmatism or impressionism, of dogmatism *and* impressionism. The new history understood scientism as a subjectivism that dared not acknowledge itself as such.

Strange coincidence: the New Criticism of the 1960s, defining itself against literary history without thinking through this contradiction, also gave the feeling that it was navigating between dogmatism and impressionism. (In any event, it has been so accused, and the issue of the two Barthes has something to do with it.)

Strange coincidence, bizarre paradox: there were two "old old criticisms" (or an ambivalence within the old), there were two "New Criticisms" (or an ambivalence within the new, like a hybrid of science and literature): it illustrates the profound intention of criticism to be in itself writing, which none disputed with Sainte-Beuve, Brunetière, or Faguet). In the meantime, between the two was literary history as straight as a die, without laying claim to literature. As if history were repeating itself for being laid aside so much, as if history were avenging itself. Isn't this flavor of repetition, this unforeseen return of the old old criticism in the new criticism, like a reincarnation, a sign that the hidden side of literary theory is in fact literary history, the history of literary history, particularly its institution against the old old criticism?

I do not mean to suggest that there was some of Brunetière and Faguet in Barthes, some of the doctrinaire *and* some of the *bel esprit*, that the two Barthes—structural analysis and pleasure of the text—are dogmatism and impressionism revisited three-quarters of a century after the fact. However, the interesting similarity between the duplicity of the old old criticism and that of the new criticism beyond literary history only begs to ask this question: why did the new criticism never speak of the old old criticism (say, Sainte-Beuve, Taine, and Brunetière) and the rise of the old criticism (say Lanson)? At what expense?

Thus my subject: to write the history of literary history (the footnotes of history), an obligation that the new criticism chose to ignore. To write the history of history in order to prevent (if possible) its repetition, a surreptitious return of the old old to the new, an eternal perpetuation of traditional literary history. All of this instead of dispensing with a reflection on literary history and witnessing passively the never-ending repetition of history; instead of haughtily refusing history with the illusion that, once thrown out the door, it will not return so soon through the window.

One might object: fine, you may study literary history, examine its problematic, explain the general discredit into which it has fallen. But why should these analyses assume the historical form?

Precisely because literary history has no determination other than historical, because it is not separable from the circumstances of its coming into being. Because it presupposes no conception of literature, because it is entirely devoted to its teaching, not only on the university level, where it seeks to transmit learning and to promote research, but on the secondary and even primary levels, eager—why not?: after all, there does not seem to be anything against it—to define, to propagate a mythology and an ideology which, under the circumstances, are republican and patriotic. Because literary history is above all an ideology (the notion of a national literature), and an ideology should first be grasped historically. Confronted with that which presents itself as self-evident—national literature and literary history—there is no other recourse but to begin by making it relative, that is, historical.

Subsidiary reason: despite the discredit of literary history in

all of its forms, how does one forgo relating history and literature? (If one wants to stay in tune with one's time.) Writing the
history of literary history is thinking for today and tomorrow.
Though outmoded in appearance, the question is of the utmost
pertinence. The beginnings of the Third Republic (particularly its
ideological aspects) are urgent for us to understand.

I am exaggerating: among the partisans of the new method, all
of them have not lost interest in history; a few have nonetheless
looked into its relationship to criticism, be it merely to conclude
that it would be better if there were none at all. Roland Barthes
was among these, only once, but once and for all, as if to settle the
score. It is not by chance that his article was entitled "History or
Literature?" and the "or" is an *aut;* he bets on a mutual exclusion
despite the rhetorical question mark. As early as 1960, Barthes
skillfully acknowledged the legitimacy of a certain literary history, in order formally to detach himself from it. Far from con-
demning every historical approach, he would map out its good
(uncontestable) program and make a severe, clear-cut, and in-
cisive distinction from his own. "In short, in literature, there are
two postulates: one is historical, insofar as literature is an institution; the other psychological, insofar as it is creation. Two disci-
plines are thus required to study it, differing both in object and
method; in the first case, the object is literary institution, the
method is historical method in its most recent developments. In
the second case, the object is literary creation; the method is psychological investigation."[2] On the one hand, the Barthes of *On
Racine*, aware as he was of psychoanalysis understood as psycho-
criticism, reserves the right to speak of the "individual" side of
literature. On the other hand, the author of *Writing Degree Zero*
and of the little *Michelet*—who could not pass for a frantic denier
of history—accuses traditional literary history of having confused the two sides of literature, institution and creation, of having
approached creation with the tools of positivist history: sources,
influences, and so forth.

But there is now a new history which was wise enough to leave
the singular events by the wayside—a battle, a man, a work—
to concentrate on repeated acts. Let this serial or social history,
Lucien Febvre's historical sociology, take responsibility for the
resolutely "collective" side of literature, the literary institution
on this side of the text, the literary functions beyond individuals:

the milieu, the audience, its intellectual formation, the facts of collective mentality, and so on. May this institutional history avoid like the plague entangling itself with the relationship between the work and its author. "Literary history," Barthes tells us, tacitly reviving Lanson's project at the turn of the century— alas! still in the state of a project—"literary history is possible only if it becomes sociological, only if it becomes interested in activities and institutions, not in individuals" (*On Racine*, p. 156). Acknowledged! But the new criticism will not be that history, loosely Marxist and inspired by the new history—it will be completely different. "Amputate the individual from the literature! One sees the uprooting, the very paradox," Barthes concludes. "But a history of literature is only possible at this price; even if it means specifying that the history of literature, brought back necessarily into its institutional limits, will be merely history."

Having foreseen the place of a history of literature completely integrated with history, having in a way covered itself on the side of history, the new criticism will wash its hands of the matter and go back to its own business. It will define itself close to if not against history, without dispute over object or method, as in the neutrality of two foreign languages; it will deploy itself with a totally clean conscience on the other side of the line: the work, the text, the individual. (Certainly not the author, who was the illusory mediation, since Sainte-Beuve, between history and literature, the center, the synthesis, the link between the work and society: the author falls through in the careful separation of history and literature, of institution and creation. This is exactly the meaning of his death: he simply has no reason to be, if the social side of literature is sent back to history, and the individual side back to theory.) And while the history of the institution, of literary functions, reaches scientific objectivity, criticism (no longer having as its object the work as historical product but as form, system of signs) is, according to Barthes, necessarily the domain of the arbitrary, commitment, the individuality of the critic himself.

To distinguish him sharply from the historian, Barthes said that the critic is "also a part of literature." The new criticism took up this refrain in unison, without ever specifying (to my knowledge) that this was already the case before 1890, before literary history set itself up against criticism—a literary genre among

others—without perhaps realizing, unless in Barthes's very astute article, that the simple act of turning one's back to history
induced this affinity beyond the break achieved by literary history. (I don't say this to reduce the originality of the claim of the
new criticism—there is no identical repetition—but to expose a
dimension which is at once theoretical and historical in its denial
of history, this historical thickness that the new criticism did not
accord itself.)

However, defining itself negatively opposite history—institutional and objective—Barthes accepts, even lays claim to (as the
very distinguishing marks of the critic), the two grievances formulated against the old old criticism of Brunetière and Faguet as
well as against the new criticism of the 1960s and 1970s: systema-
ticism *and* subjectivism, dogmatism and impressionism, apparently contradictory but united nonetheless (Brunetière's dogmatism is a sneaky impressionism, a blind subjectivism in the eyes
of Lanson, for example). The critic, if he speaks of the individual—the work and/or the creator—is committed: and so, says
Barthes, "we must accept seeing the humblest of learnings become suddenly systematic, and the most prudent critic reveal
himself as a fully subjective being, fully historical" (*On Racine*,
p. 166). I emphasize: systematic and subjective. Opposite history,
on the other side of the line, in literature, the two Barthes, the systematic and the subjective, the dogmatic and the impressionist,
the rough and the tender, the methodist and the hedonist, are
united. It is from the point of view of history—which is not so
easily disposed of, as one can see—opposite history (against history, with the ambiguity of the preposition which marks both
proximity and opposition), that Barthes is one: a "fully historical
entity."

All the more reason for writing the history of traditional literary history, alleged history of literary creation and therefore truly
committed criticism, "fully historical." To analyze it is to discover the systematic and subjective elements from which it derives its explosive mixture—it is to know it historically.

I am reducing Barthes's 1960 position to its essential: aban-
doning literary function to the historians, the new criticism de-
votes itself to forms, to their synchronic system. If it is satisfying
for the mind, such a clean division is very likely to be untenable.
Gérard Genette, in an article suitably entitled "Literature and

History"—difficult not to take it as a response—harks back to the exclusion put forth by Barthes and broadens the program of a new criticism to the dimensions of history, at the very least to those of diachrony.[3] He proposes a compromise between history and theory, something like a theoretical history or historical structuralism—that is a history of forms. In short, to focus on forms and not on literary functions, and despite its apparent denial of history, criticism, according to Genette, is nonetheless "condemned to meet history along the way." The Russian formalists had already denounced pure synchrony as illusory and undertaken the positioning of forms in time, the individual work in a literary evolution, in a succession of systems.[4] But diachrony, succession, evolution—are they sufficient to make history?

Besides, the so-called works of poetics have become, little by little but increasingly—unrelentingly—"historicized." After the apparent denial of history came its apparent revival. Take Genette or Todorov: a history of the symbol, a history of cratylism, a history of pastiche, of parody and of other plagiarisms, all this alongside theory.[5] (The history of a form is also what I attempted: the evolution, the succession of functions corresponding to a repetition of others' words.[6] A hoax because it is not this.) Taking into account the diachronic figure of a form, treating it at the intersection of a formal and a historical plan, perhaps amounts to writing the history of a form. It certainly does not mean including this form in history, to draw a relationship between literary and social series, literary forms and social functions—it is always to separate forms from history, and even more insidiously than Barthes, who at least did not mix genres.

Let's go one step further to combine, to try to combine, theoretical knowledge and historical knowledge, Marxism and formalism, the one step which Jauss took: no longer a history of forms (a poetics of production), but a history of their perception, of the effect produced by the forms (an aesthetic of reception). The reader, instead of the author, becomes the mediation between literature and society; the reader is the locus of a literary history. Through him, the forms would be in a dialectical relation to history, not only determined by history (products, mirrors, documents, according to the usual conceptions), but also active and influential, transforming the world.[7]

Aren't we going round in circles? Doesn't the history of a

form (the one Genette posited beside the historical history of functions), ally itself again with the old old criticism of Brunetière? Brunetière made his name in the evolution of literary genres. The literary genre is obviously the privileged object of a history of forms, understood as a poetics concerned with diachrony. And this was, in fact, how Brunetière saw the genre: as a link in the chain, beyond the author, between institution and creation, society and the work. The aesthetic of reception (the one Jauss proposed beside all the histories of literary production); does this not again recall Taine's notion of milieu, taken in its broadest meaning, the richest, in which it refers not only to an action of the milieu on the individual but to a dialectic connection, of sympathy or sociability, between the work and its audience? The reader, in Jauss's sense, was already for Taine the essential third.

The interdependences of history and literature are an inextricable wasp's nest (unless we reduce the work to a historical document, period, neglecting its essential paradox—that it belongs at once to history and art, whose objects never die). Despite so many advances and balks at long intervals for over a hundred years, we have now—it seems to me—progressed one inch. The cries of alarm have remained unheeded, just as the Cassandras have been shouting themselves hoarse, and history has remained a delusion of the literary critics. (The wisest thing, as Barthes indicated, would be to trace firebreaks. Unfortunately, this is impossible: history is the strongest.)

Literary history, we see, was born in reaction to the magisterial power of the historians in the French university after 1870. There are always historians to hold the power (cultural if not political). After those positivists who imposed themselves on the men of letters at the turn of the century came the *Annales* school, with whom Barthes came to terms. One of his rare articles in *Annales* was "History or Literature?" of 1960, in which he accredited social history and gave carte blanche to the descendants of Lucien Febvre to deal with the literary institution, while he kept form. He paid tribute to history, if by distinguishing himself from it with elegance. Genette also had published a historical article in *Annales*, "Enseignement et rhétorique au XIXme siècle" (Teaching and Rhetoric in the Nineteenth Century), precisely one of the only studies, and an excellent one, on the death of the rhetoric which coincided with the birth of literary history—what

I take as yet another indicator of the crucial nature of that moment for our culture.[8] Nothing better than the *Annales* represents the power of the historian during the 1960s, as Lanson wrote in the *Revue d'histoire moderne et contemporaine* in 1903. Having made a gesture of allegiance, he was elected the following year to the Sorbonne.

The "fully historical being" of the critic rests also, to a wide extent, on his determination in relation to the contemporary historians; it is through them that he meets the general historical series. (I am caricatural but there is some truth to it; as I said, I do not think that history repeats itself identically. Had these pages been published in the *Annales* or the *Revue d'histoire littéraire de la France* with the heirs of Lucien Febvre or those of Gustave Lanson, that would surely have cemented historical alliances, but would have digressed from the bearing of the topic: on the historical alliances of literary studies.)

For this history, several titles would have been possible and I have too many in mind. First this one, poetical: "La vieuvre." Because this wordplay actualizes the very concept (already quite determinist and materialist) of literary history which has not ceased exploring the relations—presumably causal—between the life (*vie*) of an author and his work (*oeuvre*). My second title, in the manner of a history of mentalities, would be: "The Invention of a Discipline." My third, parodic: "Gustave Lanson: His Life, His Work."

However, all three are unacceptable because they recall the wanderings of a history which misunderstands history. My fourth title, more circumstantial: "Essay on the Institution of Literary Studies in France, on Their Grandeur and Decadence, on the Causes of the One and the Other, on the Intellectual, Moral, and Social Atmosphere of the Time, Extended with Considerations on Flaubert and Proust, as *terminus a quo* and *ad quem*." A trifle awkward no doubt, but it says well what it means and it also introduces two writers, so as not to remain too historical.

From Flaubert to Proust: this is France without Alsace and Lorraine, this is the death of the classical rhetoric and of the humanities, the impulse of literary history while the university isolates itself from literature and criticism. From Flaubert to Proust: the "break" in the approach of literature which preceded that of the 1960s and of the new criticism. Furthermore, Flaubert and

Proust: not in order to perfect the defense and illustration of another literary history, nor to attempt yet one more time to reconcile criticism and history, but quite simply to demonstrate the coincidence between a fictional form and a historical choice.

It was abroad, in London, that I took up this quintessentially French subject: the Troisième République of the Ecole Libre and the separation of church and state, Jules Ferry's and that of the old Combes, our *Ursprung*, the France of "our ancestors the Gauls," up to us who date from after the Algerian War and May 1968. The *lycée* had not changed, the curriculum was carting the same myths: Lagarde and Michard, Malet and Isaac. Our culture has been essentially historical—hence the new criticism as something novel—and it was after us that the schools lost touch with history, with French history, that is, the history of Lavisse, leading to the Third Republic.

Singularity, however, of the selection of a patriotic, almost chauvinistic subject, "La Troisième République des Lettres," as if in the grips of a disorientation, a nostalgia, in search of a childhood memory, of roots. To tell the truth, I did not, for the most part, know the French *lycée*, which I take to be the real France, the manufacture of authentic French people. One might say: what better reason for undertaking the archaeology of childhood memories of high school students from the time when they were would-be gentlemen?; only the memories of others were desirable, and true French make fun of the Troisième République des Lettres: French ideology, they have it in their own blood and will not stop to marvel at it. Without contradicting, I insist upon the margin, the necessary distance to delve into that which appears self-evident: the great French writers, Victor Hugo, Racine, and Voltaire, proof of a national literature, for anyone who took the baccalaureate examination up through the late 1960s.

I had to cross the Channel to bring myself back, to return to our side (I have said how this possessive ought to be understood), in order to think out the difference between here and there, us and them—between literary studies in France and in England, which are completely different. Spontaneously, like a good pupil of the Troisième République des Lettres, I accounted for it by the English resistance to theory, by the absence of a structuralist conversion during the 1960s. First of all, it was the earlier shift that English literary studies never underwent: that of the 1890s which led, in France, from criticism to history. Here is the clearest sign: there is still only one educated public in London, whereas Sainte-Beuve, Taine, and Brunetière were addressing at the same time scholars and casual readers, and they were the last in France (until Roland Barthes, who also allied himself with them on this point and reconciled the two publics—the last but not least affinity). I am simplifying, but London was the opportunity to discover that literary history was not self-evident, to hunt down what is taken for "natural" in the Troisième République des Lettres, to observe that crisis from which it resulted and which the new criticism misunderstood.

Surprisingly, Proust, who argued with Sainte-Beuve at a time when the latter was outdated, is among the last writers—with Paul Bourget—for whom criticism was still literature and had not yet surrendered to history. (Proust, a legendary anglophile, would be our last typical writer of the English school.) While Flaubert, who dined regularly at Magny's with the first of critics—but also with Taine and Renan—indicated more exactly the transition from criticism to history. (Can we think of a more congenitally French writer than Flaubert?) The Troisième République des Lettres took form between Flaubert and Proust—between Proust and Flaubert, I would be tempted to say. It is also this intertwining that we must illustrate.

(That, it goes without saying, will not do. Proust is an ambiguous author, the last writer of the nineteenth or the first of the twentieth century, the last and the first. If he was unaware of history, it was—the new criticism appropriated him—as forerunner of a critical formalism. Today the friend of Taine and Renan is still made into a prophet of literary modernity.)

One might counter: "By coming back to history, you are turning away from criticism to which you had seemingly adhered until now; you are negating theory, formalism, and so on; in short, you are a traitor to the fathers to whom you owe everything."

"Not at all. Only a modernist premise can demand a historical reconsideration of literary history in order to stop the noncritical return, over literary history, of the old old criticism within the new criticism; that is, to think through this return, not at all to forbid it."

"Paradoxes!"

"And then by doing the history (of literary history), I am writing the history of history (the literary history of literary history). What more eloquent display of fidelity to the essential conventions of modernity! *Mise-en-abyme*, self-conscious autonomy, reciprocal implication of object and method. Like an *hommage*. Far be it from me to betray!"

"Sophisms and palinodes!"

"If that's all it is, we've seen it before . . ."[9]

Notes

1. Raymond Picard, *Nouvelle Critique ou nouvelle imposture?* (Paris: Pauvert, 1965); Roland Barthes, *Critique et vérité* (Paris: Seuil, 1966).

2. Barthes, "Histoire ou littérature?" *Annales* (May 1960), 524–537; *Sur Racine* (Paris: Seuil, 1963), p. 149.

3. Gérard Genette, "Littérature et histoire," in Serge Doubrovsky and Tzvetan Todorov, eds., *L'Enseignement de la littérature* (Paris: Plon, 1971), reprinted in *Figures III* (Paris: Seuil, 1972).

4. See Yuri Tynianov, "De l'évolution littéraire," in Todorov, ed., *Théorie de la littérature* (Paris: Seuil, 1965).

5. Genette, *Mimologiques* (Paris: Seuil, 1976) and *Palimpsestes* (Paris: Seuil, 1982); Todorov, *Théories du symbole* (Paris: Seuil, 1977).

6. Antoine Compagnon, *La seconde main* (Paris: Seuil, 1979).

7. See Hans-Robert Jauss, "L'Histoire de la littérature: Un défi à la théorie littéraire" (1967), in *Pour une esthétique de la réception* (Paris: Gallimard, 1978). See also Walter Benjamin, "Histoire littéraire et science de la littérature," in *Poésie et révolution* (Paris: Denoël, 1971); René Wellek, "The Concept of Evolution in Literary History," in *Concepts of Criticism* (New Haven: Yale University Press, 1963); and "The Fall of Literary History," in R. Koselleck and W. D. Stempel, *Geschichte: Ereignis und Erzählung* (Munich: Fink, 1973); A. Kibédi Varga, "L'histoire littéraire," in *Théorie de la littérature* (Paris: Picard, 1981).

8. Genette, "Enseignement et rhétorique au XIXe siècle," *Annales* (March 1966), reprinted in *Figures II* (Paris: Seuil, 1969).

9. An earlier version of sections 14, 15, and 16 of the first part appeared under the title "Comment on devient un grand écrivain français," in *Le temps de la réflexion* (Paris: Gallimard, 1982).

BETTY R.
MCGRAW

Public Parks and Private Gardens: Sartre's Nausea and Barthes's Ennui

---

The park came into existence only in order to harmonize with a certain state of mind.
— J.-P. Sartre, *What Is Literature?* (1947)

The garden, though continuous, is arranged in three symbolically different spaces . . . : the worldly, the domestic, the wild; is this not the very tripartition of social desire?
— *Roland Barthes by Roland Barthes* (1975)

Temptations

In *Nausea*, Jean-Paul Sartre studies the concept of ennui from the vantage point of a philosophy influenced by Husserl's method of bracketing the world. Defined in ontological terms in *Being and Nothingness*,[1] nausea gives us a different system of reference in which pebbles, hands, and chestnut trees function as the synecdoches of a discourse which contaminates Roquentin's very existence: "Nausea. . . , it is no longer an illness or a passing fit: it is I" (*N*, p. 170).[2] Oppressed by a world of objects, Roquentin fills his journal with essentialist signs which bring out the primacy of consciousness and portray a narrator whose ennui becomes the origin both conscious and unconscious of the novel. In *The Words*, Sartre describes nausea as a tenacious feeling which ruled his existence: "Nevertheless, boredom clung to me. At times discreetly, at times disgustingly, I yielded to the most fatal temptation whenever I could no longer bear it . . ." (*M*, p. 244). Though he dramatized this "fatal" temptation with the creation of Roquentin, Sartre was yet to discover another form of fatality, the kind that evolves from the problematical relationship between fiction and reality in his novel: "I *was* Roquentin; I used him to show, without complacency, the texture of my life. At the same time, I was *I*, the elect, chronicler of Hell, a glass and steel photomicroscope peering at my own protoplasmic juices" (*M*, pp. 251–252).[3]

Just as the alchemist transmutes metal and glass into gold, Roquentin the analyst attempts to turn the banalities of his everyday experiences into a book "hard as steel" (*dur comme de l'acier*) which would escape the problematics of time, the subject and meaning through which ennui has traditionally been analyzed. Yielding to instincts usually associated with the pleasure principle, Roquentin thus abandons his research on the biography of the marquis de Rollebon, which bored him to distraction and only added to his "mushroom existence" (*existence de champignon*) and considers writing himself (his self) as subject: "I think I'm going to have the Nausea and I feel as though I'm delaying it while writing" (*N*, p. 231). In imitating his creator's avocation, Roquentin seeks a way out of his tedious existence into the *Imaginaire* through an intentional act. But in the process of reflecting upon a medium—writing—that demands replacing essentialist signs with their structural components, Roquentin is overcome by the unsettling discovery that signs are empty, devoid of meaning and sense, and that their profusion alone cannot vindicate the truth of being. Pitted against the background of those things-as-they-are (*les existants*), Roquentin's nausea triggers a primal fear: "I was *in the way* for eternity" (*N*, p. 173). It is the excess of this affirmation which becomes the novel's *raison d'être* and unleashes a philosophical desire to explain man's truth. But unable to say anything about the ever-widening fissure within his self, Roquentin ends up keeping a diary—the very "novel" which we are now reading—as an ironic gestative in preparation of a book to come.[4]

Unlike the narrator of *Roland Barthes by Roland Barthes* who finds his "truth" in his image-repertoire, Roquentin's contemplated escape through writing has been sabotaged by an idealist's illusion.[5] In the pages which follow, I want to examine how Barthes rewrites ennui with a poetic stance which negates the existential terror of boredom expressed in Sartre's *Nausea*. Furthermore, in reframing the sociolectal image of this traditional concept (its reception within the collectivity as a whole), it is my contention that Barthes positively affirms the central value of ennui as well as its attendant ambiguities within his own *Imaginaire.*

"Bourgeoisophobia"

Roquentin's discourse on ennui is grounded in a metaphysics which indicates that he is less a splenetic Baudelairean adventurer than an existential one. Sartre describes his anxiety as "a dull and inescapable nausea [which] perpetually reveals my body to my consciousness."[6] Placing bodily concerns at the service of consciousness is a gesture denied by Barthes's notion of the writerly body. But it is essential for Sartre, for whom consciousness is the only human reality and the seat of all that is Truth. In adding *Nausea* to his ongoing philosophical inquiry into the universal substance of bourgeois existence, Sartre was prefiguring a revolt against the absurdity of reality and was beginning to define a praxis based on a rational concretion.

But our "post-age" has formulated critical tools from the intersection of psychoanalysis and structuralism. These, in turn, undermine the writer's idealistic tendencies to make a text into the transparent presentation of a continuous thought integrated into a philosophical system. What these theories tell us is that Sartre's ontological study of ennui is always (always already) caught up within the closure of a system of signs. Its origin and truth—its etymon—is primarily a question of language.[7] Barthes's writing *about* ennui always overflows the boundaries of phenomenological and existential rhetoric, spilling over as figures of a bodily sort of language. As a result, the Sartrean experience of being-in-the-world is first of all the experience of being-in-the-world-of-language. In denouncing the naturalizing operation which the petit-bourgeois ideology performs on language, Barthes returns the problem of verisimilitude to its source, that of language and of the complex relationship between words and feelings or emotions: "It can't be helped: boredom is not simple" (*PT*, p. 25).[8] Distrusting the militant imperatives of *littérature engagée*, Barthes does not attempt to put the writing of ennui at the service of an existential anterior truth: "in the classical system, such an effort would have been sanctified under the name of *authenticity*, I abandon the exhausting pursuit of an old piece of myself" (*RB*, p. 56), says he, flinging from his Paris balcony the piece of rib which had

been removed from his body during an extrapleural pneumo-
thorax surgery.

If the anguished conscience of a Sartre provides the basis for
a socio-philosophical pursuit, Barthes wrenches ennui from the
totalizing moment of idealistic philosophy and sets it within a
semiotic pursuit linked to the personal, the emotional involvement of an unknown praxis. In recasting the phenomenological
idiom with which Sartre defines nausea into the personal terms
of auto/bio/graphy, Barthes rewrites ennui in a manner that parallels the changing concept of writing and brings to light problems associated with notions of sincerity and authenticity. Speaking of *Roland Barthes*, the narrator describes it in a manner which
denies access to the classical confessional genre: "This book is not
a book of 'confessions'; not that it is insincere" (*RB*, p. 120). As far
as Barthes is concerned, the classical notions of sincerity and authenticity which require that the subject submit his reality to the
laws of the signified usher in a cultural discourse in which there is
no personal flow.

While the emphasis is on the personal, it does not follow,
however, that what Barthes wants is a drifting moral disponibil-
ity. The narrator of *Roland Barthes* states that "it is evident that
the object of all his work is a morality of the sign (*morality* is not
morale)" (*RB*, p. 97). But in taking his leave from the thinking of
groups like the Moral Majority that accept the tyranny of the signified, Barthes discards the puritanical link that exists between a
form and its obligatory meaning. One will remember Sartre denouncing the nauseating legacy of bourgeois mentalities in the famous sequence of the Bouville museum during which Roquentin
is overcome with nausea as he faces the portraits of the city's
most illustrious fathers (the *salauds*). In *Roland Barthes*, however,
the bourgeois legacy is contested by the erasure of the discursive
authority of the symbolic father. There is no longer any anxiety of
influence, no longer any metaphysical guilt or bad faith, for the
received mythologies of "familialism" are replaced by a sentimental meditation on the family photograph—a gallery of personal portraits—inserted at the beginning of the text. With the
death of the father "fallen on the field of honor" and the erasure of
his name from the school blackboard, Barthes's genealogy is cut
off from the symbolic discourse of inherited values and set adrift.

And so ennui has no need of heirs; inasmuch as it is written metaphorically, it transmits itself outside the language of the logo-theoretical father. According to the narrator of *Roland Barthes*, his work is not so much antihistorical as it is *antigenetic*, for "Origin is a pernicious [Father] figure" (*RB*, p. 142). Linking the personal to the conceptual, Barthes rewrites ennui in the traces of previous master concepts which go from the generic to the theoretical to the anecdotal, thereby drawing the new "concept" into the structural territory of the *hors-définition*. Even in those few instances when ennui retains formal sameness, it becomes comparable to the mythical ship Argo in that the only thing that remains of the original is the name. Since ennui never assumes "the definitive form of a sign grimly weighed by its signified" (*RB*, p. 98), its meaning becomes, in the eloquent words of Jacques Lacan, "always to come or withdrawn."[9] When all prior assumptions about meaning are suspended, the sign becomes exempt from the value judgments of moral and philosophical decipherments. It should be clear that, in Barthes's view, this very suspension constitutes its power. As Barthes performs upon the concept a dialectical transformation, a piece-by-piece de(re)construc-tion contrasting with the fixated position of "moral" authority, writing (on) ennui becomes a mode of action, a praxis. At the same time, this gesture must be accepted as an exemplary moral one.

Pour Rien

The ten years or so that separate Sartre from Barthes allow the latter to adopt the position of reader vis-à-vis the Sartrean oeuvre and to question Sartre's textual practice as informed by his use of the linguistic sign. Here, we might expect Barthes to define Sartre's *Nausea* as a prattling text—a text whose verbal activity is unable to generate a blissful text (*un texte de jouissance*): "I am offered a text. This text bores me. It might be said to *prattle*. The prattle of the text is merely that foam of language which forms by the effect of a simple need of writing. . . . This prattling text is then a frigid text, as any demand is frigid until desire, until neurosis forms in it" (*PT*, pp. 4–5).

Contrasting need (*le besoin*) with desire (*le désir*), Barthes negates the value of prattle with a figurative language whose openness rewrites the social and unfreezes its frigidity. One consequence of the shift from demand to desire is that Barthes's writing has become more tactical, a displacement toward a transgressive avant-garde, but one which nonetheless fixes him at the intersection of his individualist moods. This situation produces a sign of ennui whose arbitrariness he can both denounce and celebrate. Barthes notes that "it is possible to enjoy the codes even while nostalgically imagining that someday they will be abolished: like an intermittent *outsider*, I can enter into or emerge from the burdensome sociality, depending on my mood—of insertion or of distance" (*RB*, p. 131). Characteristically, when ennui is ideologically recycled, it produces a critical return, a typically Barthesian second-degree perversion—what he refers to as a "pleasure of ideology." Now a negative, now a positive value, ennui can move from the discredited notion of structure to the perverse notion of expenditure—something along the lines of Bataille's economy of the *pour rien*.

On the negative side, ennui is created through narrative structure and the existence of certain tropes. As the effect of an overdetermined narration, it authorizes a given feeling, a "reality" which borrows certain resources from the illusion of the natural. When that reality becomes self-evident, it also becomes violent: "the 'natural' is, in short, *the ultimate outrage*" (*RB*, p. 85). Discussing Grenadier Gobain's suicide, as told by Bonaparte, Barthes asks, "From what language, one wonders, did these lovesick, melancholy grenadiers draw their passion [scarcely in accord with the image of their class and profession]? What books had they read—or what stories been told?" (*RB*, p. 91). Perspicaciously, Barthes knows that "it is language which is assertive, not he" (*RB*, p. 48) and argues for a dilatory sign which would neutralize the oppressive rule of "natural" meaning.

If the figures of Barthes's ennui refuse to be imprisoned within the violence of phraseology, it is because phraseology, like the stereotype, is the place where the body is missing. In counteracting the hardening effect the Social has on the body's arterial web Barthes strews his writings with rejuvenated neologisms, *enantioseme* (i.e., "words which have the same form and contrary meanings" [*RB*, p. 62]) and "psychological kitsch." These tactical gestures produce a dynamic force (*une mouvance*) which wrenches the old categories of knowledge from their sclerotic and regressive background and brings them closer to "the body, to the drift" (*RB*, p. 84).

With the same critical turn he performed on the old category of aesthetics, Barthes subjects ennui to the movement of the spiral, producing a gradual torsion "where everything recurs, but in another, higher place: it is then the return of the difference, the movement of metaphor; it is Fiction" (*RB*, p. 89). No longer seen as a social text which dictates a truth to all, ennui claims no "truth" but evolves into a consideration of affects, becoming a tactical calculation which mitigates the reality-effect and the dangerous consequences noted above. Whereas in *Nausea* consciousness features a reduced conception of the body, ennui in Barthes's writing becomes the sign of a desire for self-knowledge which originates in the body. Once the body is acknowledged as the structuring metaphor of a personal style, ennui loses its idealistic connotation to become a critical tool for understanding the ideolectal meaning of the author's style.

Ecriture

The question of style suggests that Barthes's ennui elicits a practice of reading and writing which extends outside Sartrean philosophical exploration and beyond traditional academic criticism. For style is an uncharted language territory which enters critical discourse obliquely—through the devices which are to be found in the articulation of language and writing. Critics who are aware of Derrida's seminal work on style also know that Lacan has equally insisted on the fact that the most hidden truth manifests itself through a path which is called *a style*.[10] In his role as pedagogue, Lacan has further argued that the transmission of knowledge and the training of his adherents consist in following the stylistic path.[11] As far as he is concerned, style is what it's all about.

Now it is very unlikely that Sartre ever considered ennui as a stylistic turn structuring the process of writing and ushering in an unspeakable truth (*une vérité indicible*). Indeed, much of his *Nausea* concentrates on the use of language as the conveyor of a certain philosophical and aesthetic stance. On the other hand, the stylistic audacity with which he wrote his novel,[12] and his interest in the style of some contemporary American novelists, indicates a preoccupation with rhetorical figures which "serves to praise a new value, *writing*" (*RB*, p. 76). The fact is that Sartre's oeuvre depicts an enclitical vision of the world which spans two *epis-*

tème.[13] In the past, *Nausea* has been interpreted as the formulation of a quasipathological state, the obsessive intransigence of a philosophical code that privileges ennui theoretically and over-determines both Roquentin's actions and the reader's reactions. Indeed, *Nausea* presupposes a vigorous interlocution with a reader who is expected to become Sartre's *compagnon de route* in the struggle against bourgeois values. Other readings of this work, notably sociohistorical ones, have called for the desacralization of the romantic feeling of torment and for transforming it into a "nausea of ennui," as Flaubert calls it in his correspondence with Louis Colet. In those readings, *Nausea* becomes the expression of a physical disgust for the exhausted values of a doomed class. But a different interpretation, one similar to that suggested by Maurice Blanchot, sets *Nausea* within the dramatic experience of a subject who discovers that writing is always outside the self, an *hors-soi*.[14] Writing points to a topos without a topographia where the subject ceases to be and where, as Roquentin states, "you have to choose: live or tell" (*N*, p. 56).[15] I have already indicated that during his attempted transition from *écrivant* to *écrivain*, Roquentin is forced to confront the duplicity of the textual sign. By the same token and depending upon her interpretation of the bifacial sign, the reader may either naturalize Roquentin's nauseating existence within a contingent framework or produce knowledge of the signifier, the beginning of writing ennui as that which cannot be contained within a theoretical or explanatory discourse.

As a reader of Sartre, Barthes steps in and out of the phenomenological tradition to interrogate the impact of its "bracketing" method: "Classical phenomenology, the kind I had known in my adolescence (and there has not been any other since), had never, so far as I could remember, spoken of desire or mourning" (*CC*, p. 21). While Barthes has been steadily committed to philosophy (Barthes's posthumous *Camera Lucida* is dedicated "in homage to *L'Imaginaire* by Jean-Paul Sartre"),[16] the object of existentialism disappears behind the fictional subject in Barthes's later works and the erosion and erasure of philosophical theories create an absence which is opposed to the Sartrean notion of *engagement*. In his desire to personalize theory, Barthes turns away from the reflexive consciousness of Sartre and moves closer to an affective one that speaks of ennui differently.[17] In so doing, he displaces ennui from the external arena of a phenomenological science to the internal discourse of the Imaginary as it speaks to (and in) the subject within the context in which ennui occurs: solitude, self-discovery, absence. Caressing the surface of things rather than grasping them, Barthes recognizes ennui *differentially*, not essentially, as something which is particular and peculiar to him. Out of this differential economy, ennui emerges as a new zone of knowledge designated as the singular, and becomes integrated with the subject of the knower (the Nietzschean "What is it *for me?*").

Whereas Sartre's metaphysical realism defines ennui as the Absolutely Universal, Barthes would define it as a "Singularly Universal" science which addresses a reality that exists at the limit of the extant codes of both philosophical knowledge and public opinion and that is often referred to as the obtuse, the oblique, the existentially unique—in other words, what Lacan calls the Real (*CC*, p. 15). But if Barthes's effort to textualize boredom differs from Sartre's concretization of nausea, nevertheless, they are correlative aspects of the same human activity: writing. Caught between two codes, the writing subject is forced to confront a conflictual mode whose primary textual site is that of the garden.

Garden Variety

Roquentin's experience in the public garden is a purely operative field where ennui is dissected and isolated like a contagious disease which desocializes anyone who contracts it. "I feel so far away from them [i.e., Men]. . . . It seems as though I belong to another species" (*N*, p. 211). In the park, Roquentin's gaze comes to rest upon a world of objects, a mirror whose reflection constructs his objectified self.[18] But the mirror turns out to be rigged, and Roquentin's nearsightedness can only make out his reflected self as if it were a palimpsest scribbled over with an opaque text whose words, like nature, speak a duplicitous language: "colors, tastes, and smells were never real, never themselves and nothing but themselves" (*N*, pp. 175–176). When the tyrannical link between subject and object is finally exposed, the phenomenological apparatus collapses, wracked by the conspiring forces of surrealistic representations: "Of these relations (which I insisted on maintaining in order to delay the crumbling of the human world, measures, quantities, and directions) I felt myself to be the arbitrator; they no longer had their teeth into things" (N, p. 173). Proliferating plants and tree roots precipitate Roquentin's nausea, interrupting his deliberations and contributing to his stupefaction: "It left me breathless" (N, p. 171). Seeking a way out of his existential malaise, the narrator searches for a metalinguistic operator which would turn his particular emotion into an absolute—the Absolutely General: "And then all of a sudden, there it was, clear as day: existence had suddenly unveiled itself" (N, p. 171). But without an organic wholeness, his hoped-for epiphany is quickly demystified. For Roquentin's deviant vision—his hermeneutical gaze—encounters a dark pit which entraps the viscous imagery of his temporal existence: "the viscous puddle, at the bottom of *our* time" (N, p. 33).

In contrast to Roquentin, Barthes's narrator speaks of engulfment without solemnity; no misery engulfs him with any particular tumult ensuing, no pathos. For Barthes's subject, the abyss is a form of gentle loss and the feeling of annihilation that sweeps through him comes from the dilution of the self into the image of the other. To be sure, Sartre also speaks of annihilation. But his nothingness relates to a form of idealism which, paradoxically, is usually associated with the subject of plenitude. As if responding to Roquentin's lament, the narrator of *Roland Barthes* de-idealizes the subject by turning his gaze away from the photographs: "You never see your eyes unless they are dulled by the gaze they rest upon the mirror or the lens . . . where is your authentic body?"[19]

Nevertheless, the drama of the public park obfuscates Roquentin's desire to produce an authentic discourse and culminates with the discovery that a unified consciousness is a (philosophical) illusion—that it cannot put an end to the fragmentation of time, the subject, and meaning. Whereas Roquentin's existential material consists of an aborted time sequence,[20] the Barthesian subject would transform Roquentin's attacks of nausea into a mere *contre-temps* which is not against, but timely instead. As a present state of anxiety, it is time without the temporal: "as if [the subject] remembered time itself and only time" (FDA, p. 216).

Unable to "put it [his experience] in words" (N, p. 174), Roquentin resorts to a fragmentary mode of writing, as demonstrated at the beginning of the autobiographical journal.[21] "Undated Pages" (*Feuillet sans date*) contains erasures and gaps which illustrate the failure of the representative mode and invites comparison with the feeling of spacing characterized by *Roland Barthes*. To be sure, the aphoristic style in *Roland Barthes* suggests a different metaphysics in which Kantianism reappears with the inclusion of a *plural* subject. In Barthes's fragmentary writings, the demise of the Cartesian subject is accompanied by a devaluation of the ego which aborts the idealizing tendency to locate the autobiographer behind the novelist: "All this must be considered as if spoken by a character in a novel—or rather, by several characters."[22] In endorsing the claim of a fictitious subject, the narrator escapes the illusion of truth associated with the confessional genre and the pretensions of sincerity and authenticity with which Roquentin started his journal: "The best would be to write down events from day to day" (*N*, p. 7).

If "day to day" writing is liberated from the temporal in Barthes's work, ennui is likewise liberated from boredom through the anamneses. Resisting the external and mechanical transmission of signs, Barthes's subject draws on the image-repertoire of his solitary and hermetic world. In manipulating these *after-the-fact* scenes, the subject produces a form of ennui which has no meaning until the memory technique helps the subject recover the solitude of the secret garden.[23] Then it becomes "a fragrance without support, a texture of memory; something like a pure expenditure, [which is never recuperated] in any destiny" (*FDA*, p. 216).

Roquentin's alienation is echoed by the narrator of *Barthes by Barthes* in several fragments which range from exclusion to escape, but which also speak of exclusion *as* escape, as a voluntary leave from the languages of the Doxa. In a passage where the narrator, as a left-handed child (*le gaucher*), is asked to "normalize his body, sacrifice [his] good hand to the little society of the *lycée*" (*RB*, p. 98), exclusion exposes the coeval forces of totalitarianism and terrorism. And when, again, at the *lycée*, the child is forced to learn a language (English) other than his own mother tongue, he reenacts the drama of separation with the mother's body. Utterly Lacanian, the fragment entitled "La langue maternelle" resonates with the recasting of the Oedipal scenario as a drama about language which suggests the difficulty of surrendering that paradisiac coalescence with the maternal imago. At the same time, the fragment invokes a fictive symbiotic bliss which emphasizes the narcissistic pleasure associated with undifferentiation.

Dépaysement is the form of ennui which also includes anxiety, contrarieties, and isolation as well as nausea and panic. It is what the Barthesian subject feels in his own country when, watching television, he is stricken by a panic for being separated from a public form of language.[24] Like Roquentin, the subject often feels deceived, *de trop*, cut off from all expressions which connote an essence and a metaphysics of sense. But, unlike Roquentin, Barthes's subject turns *dépaysement* into a positive value which allows for an escape—a vacation (and, also, a *vacance*, in the French sense of "absence"). And yet absence is never sacrificed to the establishment of concepts and theories or their reification. Instead of the being-for-itself/in-itself theoretical struggle which animates existentialist writing, Barthes speaks of a "being *pour rien*." His narrator assumes his place at the inception of writing as a subject dispossessed of wordly discourse, unable to speak, but nevertheless eager to participate in the frantic play of meaning: "Meaning will tend toward its multiplication, its dispersion" (*RB*, p. 69).

In *Roland Barthes*, under the photograph of a small boy, one reads: "As a child, I was often and intensely bored. This evidently began very early, it has continued my whole life, in gusts. . . , and it has always been noticeable to others. A panic boredom, to the point of distress: like the kind I feel in panel discussions, lectures, parties among strangers, group amusements: wherever boredom *can be seen*. Might boredom be my form of hysteria?" (no page in the English edition; my emphasis).[25]

The reference to hysteria sends us back to the public garden in *Nausea* and to the scene of hysterical attacks when the narrator-author integrates ennui into a system whose style is, in the words of Barthes, "a vertical and lonely dimension of thought" (*WDZ*, p. 16). But there is a difference between the vertical dimension of Barthes's style, which is "a form with no clear destination, the product of a thrust, not an intention" (*WDZ*, p. 16), and the erectability of Sartrean language which functions within the logic of phallocratism. Sartre's discourse unfolds in the continuum of the social space of the public garden where the exhibitionist's phallic desire and its attendant fear of castration are described via the wounds and abrasions left upon the surface of the tumescent chestnut tree: "It *looked* like a color, but . . . like a bruise or a secretion, like an oozing" (*N*, p. 176).[26] An *atroce jouissance* and *horrible extase* identify the sado-masochistic discourse of *Nausea*, inscribing the subject within the Social where "boredom can be seen." In *Pleasure of the Text,* boredom is associated with a phallic form of *jouissance* and occurs whenever the subject is asked to give up a bit of his *Imaginaire* to assume the reality of the Social: "coteries, ambitions, advancements, interferences, alliances, secession, roles, powers . . ." (*FDA,* p. 17).[27] These social interactions lack the necessary spontaneity (the *punctum* of *Camera Lucida*) which indirectly produces affects: "Boredom cannot presume it is entitled to any spontaneity: there is no *sincere* boredom" (*PT,* p. 25).

On the positive side, hysteria is the place within which the discourse of Barthes's subject is elaborated, as he moves away from the phallic image of the tree and the sado-masochistic *jouissance* of the exhibitionist whose anatomy has been exposed for the young girl to *see* (here, the discursive corpus literally turns into an analogon of the body). As expected, the narrator of *Roland Barthes* prefers to recall his gentle pleasures through his image-repertoire, for it is as a young boy, in the secrecy of his private garden, that he discovers ennui's unusual referents: *body* and *absence:* "At the end [of the garden], a darker path and two hollow balls of boxwood: several episodes of prepubescent sexuality occurred here" (*RB,* no page). Soon, images of several gardens—"the worldly, the domestic, the wild"—emerge from his youth in Bayonne, where boredom was never nauseous but always adrift: "Coming home in the evening, a frequent detour along the Adour, the *Allées marines:* tall trees, abandoned boats, unspecified strollers, boredom's drift: here floated the sexuality of public gardens, of parks" (*RB,* no page).[28]

Far from conveying the phallic boredom of *Nausea,* Barthes's erotic discourse generates rhetorical effects which redefine ennui in terms of the subject's personal experiences inscribed in the text as bio-graphemes. Dominating all others is the experience of death, as Barthes's later reflexion in *Camera Lucida* originates under the sign of the mother whose photograph as a girl in the Winter Garden triggers the longest of all meditations. Representing the writer's sense of loss after the death of his mother and functioning as the ostensible catalyst for the text production, that missing photograph becomes paradoxically a *visible* death. By the same token, since the text was published posthumously, the narrator is situated ironically in the simple past, a "that-has-been" for the reader. Consonant with the Proustian *Recherche* with which it bears affective similarities, pathos for the dead (m)other and the need to write emanate from a nostalgic desire to re-create a past which is no longer the abstract notion of the philosopher, but the lived reality of the world of senses, as seen from the writer's personal history. This, then, is the Barthesian "here and now."

Visibilia

The nostalgia of *Roland Barthes* contrasts sharply with the phenomenological science which orients Barthes's earlier *Writing Degree Zero*. As a semiotician, Barthes was infatuated with the formal aspect of the sign; as a hedonist, he believed in the dilatation of its meaning, its *contre-rhétorique*.[29] In an article entitled *L'Imagination du signe*, Barthes notes that "the sign is not only the object of a particular knowledge, but also the object of a vision . . . the semiologist *sees* the sign moving in the field of signification, he enumerates its valences, traces their configuration: the sign is, for him, a sensuous idea" (*EC*, p. 209).[30] Over the years, Barthes's writing has produced a style whose projected image must be interrogated. "How do we *see* style? Perhaps every enterprise rests in this way on a *vision* of intellectual objects" (*RB*, p. 90).

Paralleling his changing vision of a science, ennui shifts from the notion of Universal myth to that of the personal Real. Because of Barthes's association with both drama and writing, this reality is acted out in stylistic arabesques against the backdrop of the secret garden. This scenographic discourse is wedged into a scientificity whose boredom Barthes had denounced in his 1977 inaugural lecture at the Collège de France and allows for the recognition of a personal style located somewhere in the body.[31] Far from relating body to consciousness, as in Sartrean analyses, body becomes a mana-word which holds an uncanny fascination for Barthes, as demonstrated by his interest in the alphabet of women posed as the letters drawn by Erté.[32] Here the term "figure" clearly relates to an organizational device in the text; its referent points to a denotative void and can only be located *fictively*, outside the novelistic form. In its most triumphant form, figuration hollows out concepts, forcing a fading of Meaning. In a manner reminiscent of Lacan's vision, many of Barthes's sentences remain suspended in meaning and become the matrix of figures which "explode, vibrate, in and of [themselves]. . . . They utter the affect, then break off, their role is filled" (*FDA*, p. 6). Without conceptualization, discourse becomes the product of an unmitigated desire whose libidinal energy is capable of generating fantasies.

If visual power constitutes the primal dimension of Barthes's phantasma discourse, it goes without saying that images also inhabit the "discourse of the others *insofar as [he] sees it*" (*RB*, p. 161). The predominant *visibilia* of Barthes's later writings allow for a different, "graphic" mode of existence where the speaking subject is *off*. Unlike Sartre's existential torment vocalized via Roquentin, Barthes's silent notion of writerly body provides an alternative to the semantic and logical codes of those "motionless phrases" (*phrases immobiles*) which characterize phenomenological science and to "this assertive language" (*ce langage assertif*) with which ennui is expressed in the texts of Sartre.

Thus, one might say that the issue is one of *representation*. Counterfeit images in the Sartrean text conspire with our institutions to make boredom. They are grounded not only in our cultural ignorance but in massive narcosis as well, where ennui contributes to its own hebetude. Even an original thinker such as Jean Baudrillard characterizes this state as "what is obscene, it is the glazed extreme of the body . . . an empty scene. . . . Nothing happens and yet we are saturated with it."[33] Striking at the glaze of representations in our contemporary culture is Barthes's fractious vision of a society refusing soporific phrases, mirror images of our general somnolence and inexorable enemies of life.

While Erté's alphabetical drawings point to the place where, for Barthes, the semiotic and the sensuous are reconciled, the gardens in Bayonne, where "according to the Greeks, tree are alphabets" (*RB*, no page), provide the narrator of *Roland Barthes* with a means to turn the solitude and ennui of his youth into a visible form: "In the child, I read quite openly the dark underside of myself—boredom, vulnerability, disposition to *despairs* (in the *plural*, fortunately)" (*RB*, no page, my emphasis).[34] The parenthetical correction emphasizes a variety which includes the digestive, migrainous, "sensual, muscular (writer's cramp), humoral, and especially: *emotive*" (*RB*, p. 60) and exposes "the inconsistency of the [Barthesian] subject, his atopia" (*RB*, p. 86).

Wearing various masks and speaking in many codes, this plural subject projects a fictional story, a discourse based on loss and absence, and emerges as an uncanny other whose concomitant image is of a solitary and incomplete self. As such, ennui becomes a second text which stages the play of the me-I (*le jeu du je*), putting into question the mimetic representation which governs the traditional use of pronouns and replacing them with the markings "that are gathered together under the very device of the Mirror and its Image: *Me, myself, I*" (*RB*, p. 105). Curiously, it is in the garden of Bayonne that the narrator engages in a solitary game of words in which he does not have the last word: "Bets are not placed, there can still be a game" (*Il faut que les jeux ne soient pas faits, qu'il y ait un jeu* is the French original needed here to give the quote its full impact [*PT*, pp. 4 and 11]). Denying the representative mode which governs Sartre's *Les jeux sont faits*,[35] Barthes's ennui emanates from the play of forms, from an intricate interaction among all forms which cannot be reduced to a single, specific code: "I am . . . merely a field, a vessel for expansion . . . [where] antipathetic codes (the noble and the trivial, for example) come into contact" (*PT*, pp. 5–6).

Meteorology

If the public *square* of Bouville frames and contains Roquentin's panic boredom, the Bayonne parks of Barthes's youth harbor all the exterior signs of pleasure and drift: swings, monkey bars, trains, and carousels. Emblematic of a desire to free the subject from any form of constraints associated with the history of Western metaphysics, the *manège* projects ennui's discourse away from its axial grounding, its essence or existence: "I am the story which happens to me: freewheeling in language" (*RB*, p. 56). As such, the spinning wheel conjures up the effects—albeit expanded and accelerated—of an earlier metaphor, that of the turnstile in "Myth Today," inasmuch as Barthes's writing always anticipates the simultaneous deployment of both aspects of the sign—the signifier *and* the signified. Thus, Barthes may have deplored the fixed use of Western instruments for public reference and of language coercion, but he nevertheless recognized the parergonal necessities that are grounded in the structured principle of mimesis. While repudiating ennui in its philosophical or clinical uses, he nonetheless proclaimed the affirmation of its effect. And, in so doing, his refusal to couch into a representative mode the mnemonic object of the private garden in Bayonne will continue to undermine Sartre's symbolization of the outside park which overdetermines Roquentin's feeling of nausea: it may rain in Bouville tomorrow, but will it rain in Bayonne?

Notes

1. Sartre, *Being and Nothingness* (New York: Philosophical Library, 1956); see, in particular, chapter 1 of part 2, entitled "Immediate Structures of the For-Itself," pp. 73–107. Nevertheless, it should be noted that *La nausée* is endowed with romantic overtones. One such case occurs at the end of the novel, when Roquentin uses the metaphor of the lighthouse flashing in the darkness of the night to express the activities of self-search and adventure: "La première qui s'alluma fut celle du phare Caillobotte. . . . Alors je sentis mon coeur glonflé d'un grand sentiment d'aventure" (p. 81).

2. Throughout this article, when available, I use English translations with the page number in parentheses referring to the edition in English. Used throughout this article are Jean-Paul Sartre, *La nausée* (Paris: Gallimard, 1938), Livre de Poche edition; *Nausea* (*N*) (London: Purnell and Sons, 1949), trans. Lloyd Alexander; Sartre, *Les mots* (Paris: Gallimard, 1964), collection "Folio"; *The Words* (*M*) (New York: George Braziller, 1964), trans. Bernard Frechtman; Roland Barthes, *Roland Barthes par Roland Barthes* (Paris: Seuil, 1975), collection "Écrivains de toujours"; *Roland Barthes* (*RB*) (New York: Hill and Wang, 1977), trans. Richard Howard; Barthes, *Fragments d'un discours amoureux* (Paris: Seuil, 1977); *A Lover's Discourse* (*FDA*) (New York: Hill and Wang, 1978), trans. Richard Howard; Barthes, *Le plaisir du texte* (Paris: Seuil, 1973); *The Pleasure of the Text* (*PT*) (New York: Hill and Wang, 1975), trans. Richard Miller with a note by Richard Howard; Barthes, *Essais critiques* (Paris: Seuil, 1964); *Critical Essays* (*EC*) (Evanston: Northwestern University Press, 1972), trans. Richard Howard; Barthes, *Le degré zéro de l'écriture* (Paris: Seuil, 1953 and 1972); *Writing Degree Zero* (*WDZ*) (London: Jonathan Cape, 1967), trans. Annette Lavers and Colin Smith; Barthes, *La chambre claire* (Paris: Gallimard, Seuil, 1980); *Camera Lucida* (*CC*) (New York: Hill and Wang, 1981), trans. Richard Howard.

3. In a superbly original book, George H. Bauer demonstrates that *Nausea* is Sartre's way of putting his philosophical preoccupations into an artistic form and discusses the ambiguous relationship between fiction and reality; cf. *Sartre and the Artist* (Chicago: University of Chicago Press, 1969). Along these lines, the article by Karin Gundersen entitled

"Les aventures extraordinaires d'Antoine Roquentin," *Revue Romane* 17/2 (1982), 64–74, is also of interest.

4. Roland Barthes: "the work is never anything but the metabook (the temporary commentary) of a work to come which, *not being written*, becomes this work itself" (*RB*, pp. 174–175).

5. As Blanchot states, Roquentin's reality, "c'est le glissement entre ce qui est et n'est pas sa vérité, un pacte avec l'illusion"; cf. "Les romans de Sartre," in *La part du feu* (Paris: Gallimard, 1949), p. 196.

6. *Being and Nothingness*, p. 632. While used by Julian Barnes to describe Flaubert's antics, "bourgeoisophobia" is equally applicable to both Sartre and Barthes; cf. *Flaubert's Parrot* by Julian Barnes (New York: McGraw-Hill, 1984). I am grateful to Steve Ungar for having mentioned this wonderful little book—a perfect safety valve for the intellectual's steam engine.

7. Cf. *Roland Barthes*, p. 139, and also the fragment entitled "Etymologies" in *Roland Barthes*, p. 88 (p. 85 in the English edition). Furthermore, in *Eléments de sémiologie*, Roland Barthes demonstrates how reality does not pre-exist language, fiction, or thought: "Il paraît de plus en plus difficile de concevoir un système d'images ou d'objets dont les signifiés puissent exister en dehors du langage . . . le monde des signifiés n'est autre que celui du langage" (p. 80). This idea is pursued in modernized form in his *Roland Barthes*, in the fragment entitled "La dénotation comme vérité du langage," p. 71 (p. 67 in the English edition).

8. Cf. his *Mythologies*, particularly the section entitled "Myth Today."

9. Cited by Jean-Michel Palmier, *Lacan* (Paris: Editions Universitaires, 1972), p. 13.

10. Cf., in particular, his *Eperons: Les styles de Nietzsche* (Paris: Flammarion, 1978); translated as *Spurs/Eperons* by Barbara Harlow (Chicago: University of Chicago Press, 1979).

11. In "Psychoanalysis and Its Teaching," in *Ecrits*, p. 458.

12. Among the many examples one could cite which depict Sartre's obsession with words is the tramway scene in *Nausea*.

13. This point is also made by Michael Scriven, *Sartre's Existential Biography* (London: MacMillan Press, 1984), when he says that Sartre's writing "spans two historical epochs and that his literary project is relevant to both" (p. 28).

14. The expression is by Maurice Blanchot (*La part du feu*). As is well known, in a similar fashion Derrida, taking his lead from Heidegger, places Being under erasure to emphasize the distanciation of the self from the self.

15. In *writing* these words, it could be said that Sartre privileges the role of the voice and the phonetic substance in matters of the mind as a result of a strong Husserlian influence. But Husserlian transcenden-

talism has since been deconstructed by Derrida in his seminal *Grammatology*. Therefore, it is as a "form of writing" that I am, here, using *raconter*.

16. On this matter, see the excellent study of Gary Shapiro in this collection.

17. His astute reflection goes as follows: "aussitôt prise dans le rassessement des images, elle ne tourne jamais en réflexivité: exclu de la logique" (immediately absorbed in the mulling over of images, it never turns into reflexivity: excluded from logic; *FDA*, p. 71, p. 59).

18. On one of the pages of the pictorial preface that introduces *Roland Barthes*, but on a page which is to be noted for the absence of any photograph, one reads: "Vous êtes le seul à ne pouvoir jamais vous voir qu'en image . . . vous êtes condamné à l'imaginaire" (You are the only one who can never see yourself except as an image . . . you are condemned to the repertoire of [body] images; p. 40, no page).

19. The French edition reads as follows: "vous ne voyez jamais vos yeux, sinon abêtis par le regard qu'ils posent sur le miroir ou sur l'objectif. . . . Où est votre corps de vérité?" This is precisely what Barthes does with the photographs of *La chambre claire (Camera Lucida)*, in which the gaze of the subject is confronted with the "unreal" material of absence and of love. The quotation is taken from the preface of *Roland Barthes* (p. 40 in the French edition).

20. As Blanchot states "Le mot ne peut jamais être maîtrisé ni même saisi . . . écrire, c'est se livrer à la fascination de l'absence du temps" (*La part du feu*).

21. In a recent presentation on Heidegger, Beckett, and Sartre at the Midwestern Modern Language Association (1988), Lance St. John Butler astutely traces Roquentin's nausea, as he gazes at the naked being of the chestnut tree, to the Heideggerian distinction between *Vorhanden* and *Zuhanden*. When *Vorhanden* (ready-to-hand) breaks down and becomes unusable (or unintelligible), it relapses into a mere *Zuhanden* (present-at-hand). It is this falling out of *Dasein*'s proximate world that makes the merely present-at-hand incapable of having a significant world and is, therefore, the origin of Roquentin's malaise.

22. The caption is handwritten inside the bookcover, in both the French and the English editions, and repeated on page 123 of the French edition and on page 119 of the English one. This is quite a departure from Sartre's declaration noted above whereby he leaves no doubt as to the nature of his relationship with Roquentin.

23. Speaking about psychoanalytical anamnesis, Lacan states, "it is not a question of reality, but of truth, because the effect of full speech is to reorder past contingences by conferring on them the sense of necessities to come, such as they are constituted by the little freedom through which the subject makes them present" (*Ecrits*, p. 48).

24. Cf., in *Roland Barthes*, the fragments entitled "The Fear of Language," and "The Mother Tongue," pp. 114–115.

25. *RB* (p. 28 in the French edition), which reads: "Enfant, je m'ennuyais souvent et beaucoup. Cela a commencé visiblement très tôt, cela s'est continué toute ma vie, par bouffées. . . , et cela s'est toujours vu. C'est un ennui panique, allant jusqu'à la détresse: tel celui que j'éprouve dans les colloques, les conférences, les soirées étrangères, les amusements de groupe: partout où l'ennui peut se voir. L'ennui serait-il donc mon hystérie?" (my emphasis).

26. Italic in the text.

27. As part of his distinction between pleasure and *jouissance*, Barthes berates the latter whenever it becomes "une figure fixe, violente, crue, quelque chose de . . . musclé, tendu, phallique" which necessarily leads to boredom. One must never "s'en laisser accroire par l'image de la jouissance" (*Le plaisir du texte*) [Paris: Seuil, 1973], p. 42).

28. On page 21, in the French edition, which reads: "Souvent, le soir, pour rentrer, crochet par les Allées marines, le long de l'Adour: grands arbres, bateaux en déshérence, vagues promeneurs, dérive de l'ennui: il rôlait là une sexualité de jardin public."

29. Cf. Antoine Compagnon's article "The Two Barthes," in this collection.

30. "Le signe n'est pas seulement l'objet d'une connaissance particulière, mais aussi d'une *vision* . . . le sémiologue *voit* le signe se mouvoir dans le champ de la signification, il dénombre ses valences, trace leur configuration: le signe est pour lui une idée sensible" (*EC*, p. 210; author's italics). Interestingly enough, "vision" is not italicized in the English edition.

31. In his inaugural lecture for the Collège de France, Barthes speaks of replacing the boredom of a *savoir* based on the Cartesian thinking subject with the more esculent notion of *saveur;* cf. *Leçon* (Paris: Seuil, 1978), p. 21.

32. Cf. his *Roland Barthes*, p. 130.

33. Jean Baudrillard, "What Are You Doing after the Orgy?" *Artforum* 22/2 (October 1983), 43.

34. On page 26 in the French edition, which reads: "dans l'enfant, je lis à corps découvert l'envers noir de moi-même, l'ennui, la vulnérabilité, l'aptitude aux désespoirs (heureusement pluriels)" (my emphasis).

35. A scenario published in Paris by Nagel (1947).

Signs

of

the Other

DESIRE AND RESISTANCE

LAWRENCE D.
KRITZMAN The Discourse of Desire and
the Question of Gender

---

*In place of hermeneutics we need an erotics of
art.* —Susan Sontag, *Against Interpretation* (1964)

*In what he writes, each protects his own sexu-
ality.* —Barthes, *Roland Barthes* (1975)

Barthes's rhetoric of sexuality transcribes the text as a body im-
bued with libidinal energy and capable of generating fantasies
through a figurative language that articulates theoretical fictions.
As it delineates these critical texts, writing aspires to the status of
matter. What Barthes terms the "grain of the voice"—the "materiality of the body speaking its mother tongue" (*RF*, p. 270)—
comes to signify how the body speaks in writing through verbal
choreographics which involve positions of passion, its drives,
controls, and rhythms.[1] "Figuration is the way in which the erotic
body appears (to whatever degree and in whatever form that may
be) in the profile of the text" (*PT*, pp. 85–86).

The Barthesian subject "essays" the languages of culture (art,
literature, music, photography, and food) and through that process searches for the laws of its own desire. The writer's critical
discourse links the sensuous and the conceptual in a phenomenal
relation that ultimately becomes a form of self-knowledge: "What
is significance? It is meaning, insofar as it is sensually produced"

(*PT*, p. 61). Subjectivity is indeed a rhetorical effect that is related to the body's gesture, a metaphoric bond between the graphic and the corporeal which transcribes figures of drive and defense in the spectacle of writing. The text takes the form of an erotic body with which the writing subject, who sees language and is sensitive to its figurative choreographics, has a relationship that reconciles semiotic analysis with the languages of love. Accordingly, writing rages against literal meaning and conveys, as he puts it, "pulsional incidents . . . language lined with flesh, a text where we can hear the grain of the throat, the patina of consonants, the voluptuousness of vowels, a whole carnal stereophony . . . the articulation of the body" (*PT*, p. 66). This linguistic enterprise occurs whenever the epistemological metaphors of cultural analysis inscribe the corporeal within the textual and thereby produce a scriptural practice that attests to the implicit sexuality of all language.[2]

For Barthes, the signifying process exemplifies the libidinal energy of phenomenal experience only by means of psychic tropes through which the aesthetic and the sexual coalesce to stage a critical act transforming the abstract into the sensually concrete. By ascribing value to theoretical fictions whose rhetoric constitutes allegories of sexuality, Barthes transforms analytical narrative into a reflection on desire ("a flush of pleasure" [*RB*, p. 103]) that is indeed accepted as an exemplary moral gesture. This critical writing not only functions as a wedge against science, but attests to the joy of a libidinally playful writer whose scriptural activity is charged with configurations of narcissism and is fashioned according to the exigencies of the Imaginary: "Nothing is more depressing than to imagine the Text as an intellectual object (for reflection, analysis, comparison, mirroring, etc.). The text is an object of pleasure" (*SFL*, p. 7).

Barthes's sexualization of theory is essentially a discourse of unmitigated desire set forth in the absence of the father and realized as a struggle against the constraints of literal meaning.[3] Even during his period of pseudo-scientific positivism of the 1960s, Barthes advanced the hypothesis that the birth of narrative is contemporaneous with the story of Oedipus. The loss of the Oedipal master narrative would be the end of storytelling and writing in the figurative sense. It would ostensibly signify the absence of the anxious desire for the disappearance of the father in all its multifarious manifestations: "Death of the Father would deprive literature of many of its pleasures. If there is no longer a Father, why tell stories? Doesn't every narrative lead back to Oedipus? Isn't storytelling always a way of searching for one's origin, speaking one's conflicts with the Law, entering into the dialectic of tenderness and hatred?" (*PT*, p. 47).[4] The plot of the Oedipal myth overdetermines the production of a cultural discourse characterized as antimimetic, fictive, and driven by a free-flowing psychic energy that swerves away from the threat of castration. In order to transcribe these theoretical fictions, the idealized absence of closure that exists under Oedipus must be regarded as a theoretical given. The critical fictions put forth by Barthes should be seen as creating metaphoric artifacts for a desire that is incited by the real and whose ultimate goal is to return to a paradisiac pre-Oedipal state in an effort to undermine the Symbolic order of difference.

Throughout his critical writing, Barthes's erotic relationship with language is trapped within instinctual drives. The pleasure of reading is a deeply sensual practice that is marked by the diacritical distinction between pleasure and *jouissance*. As early as *Writing Degree Zero* (1953), Barthes characterizes the libidinal qualities of Flaubert's writing as containing a perlocutionary force which arouses an intense excitation enabling the reader to journey from linguistic reality to the realm of the senses: "A rhythm of the written word which creates a sort of incantation and which, quite unlike the rules of spoken eloquence, appeals to a sixth, purely literary, sense, the private property of producers and consumers of Literature" (*WDZ*, p. 65). If pleasure is conceived as an institutional norm that emanates from cultural competence and is "linked to the comfortable practice of reading," then *jouissance* is that felicitous and unpredictable delight that violates the reader's horizon of expectations and transports him into an orgasmic state that "hysterically affirms the void of bliss" (*PT*, p. 22).

Barthes's erotics of reading attributes to the text the capacity to satisfy the dialogic need for a relationship in which the reader is already addressed by the text and is, in fact, an element of its interpretation. For Barthes, the text attends to the transitory needs of a plaintive and restless reader whose object of desire is indeed a new but different contact realized through an act of scriptural "cruising" in which the sentence is a kind of wink beckoning the reader. The text gives life to the reader's desire only through the effectiveness of its own rhetorical strategies of seduction: "To read is to make our body work . . . at the invitation of the text's signs, of all the languages which traverse it and form something like the shimmering depth of the sentence" (*RL*, p. 31). Reading is therefore an activity which recognizes the text's call for recognition as well as its power to cathect with the reader: "The sensual is always readable: if you want to be read, write sensually" (*SE*, p. 67).

By placing particular emphasis on the way writing manipulates the reader, Barthes draws our attention to the text's struggle to keep desire alive—"the metonymic pleasure of all narration" (*RL*, p. 40)—as a strategy for slowing the irreversible movement toward closure. Desire indeed becomes the object of reading since it compels us to come to grips with the promises and annunciations that narratives put forth. The act of reading is an adventure in which the reader is both an amorous and mystical subject marked by a disengagement from the external world and a subsequent adherence to the exigencies of an image-repertory produced within the hermetic world of self-love.

In another sense, however, reading becomes an act of nurturance when the reader, overtaken by a narcissistic urge, retreats from reality. Here the book is taken as a love-object, a Gestalt with which the reader identifies. Like the relationship between the child and the maternal imago as originary identification, the reader locates the Imaginary in the pleasures of the text perceived as an image of bodily unity that consists in "nursing his dual relation with the book (i.e. with the Image), by shutting himself up alone with it, fastened to it, like the child fastened to the mother and the Lover pouring over the beloved's face" (*RL*, p. 39).[5] This paradisiac coalescence of subject and image functions in a manner analogous to that of a mirror. Accordingly, it transmits the joy of a reading subject engaged in a fiction of corporeal integrity. But this dream of symbiotic bliss is also capable of yielding to a drama of separation through which the image of reading can conquer the reading subject and imbue him with the will to write. Thus, we are led to "desire the desire" the author had for the reader when he was writing. Reading therefore becomes the very catalyst of narrative production with the origin of the story located in the Other: "the (consumed) product is reversed into production, into promise, into desire for production, and the chain of desire begins to unroll, each reading being worth the writing it engenders to infinity" (*RL*, p. 41). Ultimately, writing becomes the trace of the act of reading inspired and produced as an effect of writing.

The visual arts afford Barthes the opportunity to study women as semiotic objects mediated by shaped or mastered languages. In a preface to a collection of drawings by the fashion designer Erté (Romain de Tirtoff), Barthes examines the female figure as a morphemic unit sketched out by the interplay between the graphic qualities of the letter and the sensuous contours of the body. In drawing upon the mythological stereotypes associated with the image of the woman in Western culture, Barthes characterizes Erté's conception of the female body as a fetishized textual object. Each letter of his alphabet represents a synecdoche of femininity inscribed within the silhouette of writing. Unlike the conventional concept of the fetish as a fragment severed from the whole body, it here takes on new meaning in the form of a cultural artifact submitted to the mortifying gesture of a totalized harmonious figuration. "Woman entirely socialized by her adornment, adornment stubbornly 'corporeified' by Woman's contour" (*RF*, p. 108).

The silhouette becomes a fetish for Barthes because the corporeal part object and vestimentary image merge as a composite whole that links the ornamental and the bodily in an erotic albeit paradoxically desexualized relationship. Upon closer inspection, it seems that Barthes's gaze is drawn to Erté's gynecography by the violence through which the female body is dismembered and subsequently integrated into a series of discrete units belonging to an alphabetic order mediated by a graphic materiality. "Nor is Erté's Woman a symbol, the renewed expression of a body whose forms would preserve the fantasmal impulses of its creator or its reader (as in the case with the Romantic Woman of painters and writers): she is merely a cipher, a sign referring to a conventional femininity (the stake of a social pact), because she is a pure object of communication, information, transition to the intelligible, and not the expression of the sensuous: these countless women are not portraits of an idea, fantasmal experiments, but instead the return of an identical morpheme . . ." (*RF*, p. 105). In a very real sense, Barthes sees Erté as fitting women into the coherent structure of an intelligible signifying system. At the same time, he discovers her derivative function within that system by submitting her body to the grammatical exigencies of a highly aestheticized language in which women are situated at the locus of graphic abstraction: "The signifying point of departure, in Erté, is not Woman (she becomes nothing, if not her own coiffure—she is the simple cipher of mythic femininity)—it is the Letter" (*RF*, p. 114). The semiotician therefore discovers in the female body a decorative relic, a verbal icon liberated from the occult forces of the erotic by linguistic functions that legitimize the obliteration of her libidinal power. The desexualization of the female body is more than a turning away from femininity; it represents a sterilized object of play whose true value emanates from the utopic space of a two-dimensional image.

What draws Barthes to the *Physiologie du goût* is undoubtedly the amorous relation which Brillat-Savarin maintained with a language that can literally be characterized as that of a *gourmand*. Gastronomist and semiotician alike desire words in their material presence and consequently establish a fetishistic relationship with language which represents the oral aspirations of the psychic body.[6] "B. S. desires the word as he desires truffles, a tuna omelette, a fish stew; like any neologist, he has a fetishistic relation to the individual word, haloed by its very singularity" (*RL*, p. 259). Orality is evoked here because it enables Barthes to project via analogical metaphors the sexual onto the verbal. As a result, he transforms language into discrete physical objects capable of enacting libidinal functions; orality is but an exercise of language that actualizes the pleasures of the body: "we know how insistent modernity has become, revealing the sexuality concealed in the exercise of language: to speak under certain constraints or certain alibis . . . is an erotic act (the concept of orality) . . . B. S. here furnishes what his brother-in-law Fourier would have called a transition: that of taste, oral as language, libidinal as Eros" (*RL*, p. 259).

Barthes's discussion of Brillat-Savarin situates the erotic locus of both food and language in the same bodily organ, the tongue, without which there would be neither taste nor speech: "To eat, to speak, to sing (need we add, to kiss?) are operations which have the same site of the body for the origin" (*RL*, p. 258). The economy of desire adheres to the exigencies of a linguistic appetite which produces a delight which is diffuse and yet totally permeates the sensations of our internal body through the very movements of the tongue. Language is indeed an element of erotic nurturance, with food acting as the gustative metaphor of a narrative that develops in time. Somewhat in the manner of a narrative, or of a language temporalized, taste knows surprises and subtleties—these are the perfumes and fragrances, constituted in advance, so to speak, like memories: nothing would have kept Proust's madeleine from being analyzed by Brillat-Savarin (*RL*, p. 251). Like the field of discourse which is subject to the action of degrees, gustative sensations produce meaning subsequent to their first reception and ironically evoke the pleasures of reference just when they appear to trace their very absence. Here Barthes's analysis uncovers an erotics of the table, the voluptuous effects of cenesthesia which exemplifies an idealized desire that is destined to produce euphoria and yet remain incomplete. This unsatisfied wish perhaps accounts for the paradoxical nature of unelaborated desire. Like a dream, it is built on felicitous memories evoking an intense pleasure devoid of any real sensuality while remaining on the threshold of joyful expectations: "When I have an appetite for food, do I not imagine myself eating it? And, in this predictive imagination, is there not the entire memory of previous pleasures? I am the constituted subject of a scene to come, in which I am the only actor" (*RL*, p. 264).

If ideality is an issue in Barthes's critical fictions, his essays on romantic song—and on Schumann's *Lieder*, in particular—recall a world in which desire and its object were once continuous. In these texts, musicality becomes a mode of figurative language for a subject who seeks asylum in the narcissistic pleasure of internalized bliss. Emphasizing the delight of the original dyad, Barthes glorifies the desire to preserve the unravished purity of illusion whereby the subject is engaged in the undifferentiated unity of symbiotic dependency. To sing in the romantic voice is indeed an act that is self-consuming and capable of producing a mode of orgasmic pleasure which enables the ideal and the real to coalesce in the body of desire; romantic song is a performative act that assigns to the psychic body the function of mediator of dreams: "All romantic music, whether vocal or instrumental, utters the song of the natural body: it is a music which has a meaning only if I can always sing it, in myself, with my body . . .

For to sing, in the romantic sense, is this: fantasmatically to enjoy my unified body" (*RF*, p. 288).

While the love song presupposes an imaginary interlocution, it indeed emanates from a loss that is the result of an absent other. The subject is forced to seek refuge in a musical form that is "continually taking refuge in the luminous shadow of the Mother" (*RF*, p. 298) and consequently disengages the self from the constraints of Oedipalization. The phantasmal rhythms of romantic song produce the illusion of a narcissistic fulfillment through an art that is appearance without reality: "Fantasieren: at once to imagine and to improvise: in short, to hallucinate, i.e., to produce the novelistic without constructing a novel" (*RF*, p. 291). In renouncing the semblance of referentiality, the love song fantasy engages the singer in a mode of figurative expression that marks a certain sensitivity to the institution of the novel.[7] It also affirms that art can reshape matter through form, reality through the openness of music as a nostalgic quest that is "a pure wandering, a becoming without finality" (*RF*, p. 291). The singing subject dramatizes the relation with the Other inasmuch as it becomes the ostensible catalyst of his very own sense of loss: "I struggle with an image, which is both the image of the desired, lost other, and my own image, desiring and abandoned" (*RF*, p. 290).

What is remarkable about Barthes's essay on romantic song is its exemplary allegorization of a discourse of desire which refuses the demands of the symbolic order and opts instead for pre-Oedipal bliss. Barthes's encomium of the *Lieder* is catalyzed by the will to transcend the Oedipalized typology of the opera lyric and the need to (re)discover the dream of omnipotence in a romance of union represented as a conflict-free relation liberated from the laws of gender overdetermination: "In our Western society, through the four vocal registers of the opera, it is Oedipus who triumphs . . . It is precisely these four family voices which the romantic lied, in a sense, forgets: it does not take into account the sexual marks of the voice, for the same lied can be sung by a man or a woman, no vocal 'family,' nothing but a human subject,—unisexual, one might say, precisely insofar as it is amorous: for passion, romantic love—is no respecter of sexes or of social roles" (*RF*, p. 287).

The passionate romantic love that Barthes alludes to is one that has not encountered the trials and tribulations of difference.

It reflects the desire for a primary relationship of narcissistic wholeness in which the other and the one are the same without attributes recognizable as either specifically masculine or feminine: "In short, the lied's interlocutor is the Double—my Double, which is Narcissus: a corrupt double, caught in the dreadful scene of the cracked mirror" (*RF*, p. 290). This narcissistic overestimation in the case of object-choice reveals not only a regression to the realm of the Imaginary, but also the apparent need to invent a world of neutral gender in which the body is, nevertheless, bound up with the rhythms of the semiotic. Perhaps the most revealing of Barthes's critical fictions is the notion of the text which is described as a fetishistic object of pleasure in which the "devirilized" son loses himself in the web of the maternal body.[8] The writer-child engages in an erotic activity in which the joyful pleasure derived from playing with the mother's body is but a colonization and merging with that body. The distance between mother and son has been reduced to catastrophically narrow proportions whereby the latter is fatally drawn into the vertiginous path of Arachne's labyrinth.[9] We are now emphasizing, in the tissue, the generative idea that the text is made, is worked out in a perpetual interweaving lost in this tissue—this texture—the subject unmakes himself, like a spider dissolving in the constructive secretions of its web (*PT*, p. 64). For Barthes, then, the writing subject develops the ability to become that "beautiful land" through the loss of its opacity, symbolized by the mother's body, and thus merge with the vanished corpus of childhood bliss.

However, the body in question here represents not the mother's invention, but rather the child's drama of artistic creation. Barthes's text transcribes the mother as object of scriptural production and not as its dynamic subject: "The writer is someone who plays with the mother's body . . . in order to glorify it, to embellish it, or in order to dismember it, to take it to the limit of what can be known about the body" (*PT*, p. 37). In passing from passive to active persona, the Barthesian subject—in actualizing a Kleinian intertext—reappropriates the maternal body which was destroyed in fantasy.[10] He actively remodels it through a creative act—"The hand intervenes . . . to gather and intertwine the inert threads" (*S/Z*, p. 166)—which is but a sublimated version of the urge for reparation. To be sure, the impulse to satisfy the mother is inextricably linked to the symbolic recreation of the maternal body by a male writer who paradoxically feminizes himself through the symbolic representation of the fetishistic female braid which the text emblematizes in its very materiality. Thus, in characterizing the maternal body as "what can be braided" (*RF*, p. 109), the Barthesian subject ascribes to the scriptural act the masturbatory pleasures associated with narcissistic drives. The writing of the text embodies the transgression of the forbidden satisfaction derived from the maternal. Yet it exercises an obsessional attraction for a self which paradoxically becomes a substitute object of nurturance that sustains the order of the Imaginary.

In order for the text to keep the fiction-making machine alive, its most fundamental law within Barthes's critical fantasy must be to render the satisfaction of desire incomplete. The fictional must outwit the death drive of the pleasure principle. The enactment of narrative produces a discourse of desire which represents temporality as the deferral of meaning. The writing of the text transforms a reflection on desire into a kind of resonance of language that erases the object of its articulation. Barthes's concept of the text openly thematizes the inability to repress castration and with it the refusal to incarnate the Law.

Accordingly, the braiding of the pubic hair, as it is evoked by the Barthesian subject, enacts the fable of his demands. It is a mere metaphor for the symbolic positioning of desire and the denial of castration. Like the child who arrives at the fetishistic solution as the only means to defeat the castration threat, the theorist opts for the cacophony of mutually interfering sign systems as a way to perpetuate the exigencies of desire: "We know the symbolism of the braid: Freud, considering the origin of weaving, saw it as the labor of a woman braiding her pubic hairs to form the absent penis. The text, in short, is a fetish; and to reduce it to the unity of meaning, by a deceptively univocal reading, is to *cut the braid*, to sketch the castrating gesture" (*S/Z*, p. 160). To cut the braid is thus tantamount to halting the drive and the kinetic energy that is the source motivating desire. The suspension of meaning activates the euphoria derived from an eroticized language which resists the quiescence of a castrative hermeneutics: "In him the desire for the word prevails, but this pleasure is partly constituted by a kind of doctrinal vibration" (*RB*, p. 74).

In effect, Barthes's notion of the text represents the desire to escape the fate of monumentalization and to transcend the limits of interpretation as well as the problems of classification. The notion of organic totality must be fractured in order to produce a feeling of ecstasy emanating from the site of a loss. A seam, a cut, or a discontinuity in the textual fabric stimulates the erotic energy of the reader whose affective sensibilities are attuned to the rhetoric of fragmentation. As Barthes claims, a naked body is infinitely less erotic than the spot where the garment gaps. The fragmented corpus which constitutes an ideal representational mode entices the reader and transports him into the realm of the senses: "When I try to produce this short writing, in fragments, I put myself in the situation of an author who will be cruised by the reader. It is the happiness of chance, but chance that is wished-for, quite thought-out; spied upon, in a way" (*GV*, p. 231). Barthes's *corps morcelé* enacts the fantasy of his own body in bits and pieces, a corporeal pose that implies a certain loss of self and seduces because of this very absence.

Roland Barthes by Roland Barthes sets forth an unquestionably idealistic view of sexuality that attempts to transcend the psychic mythology of the binary prison through a process of self-negation: "He dreams of a world which would be exempt from meaning" (*RB*, p. 87). The concept of the neuter becomes a scriptural metaphor in the quest to transcend the integrity of meaning in language and the threat of reification due to taxonomies. Barthes therefore problematizes the possibility of essentialized gender identities and suggests that the very idea of a "happy sexuality" can only become possible when sexual difference is disavowed. In essence, Barthes seemingly refuses those identities of man and woman as fictions of oppression imposing closure. Within this context, sexuality is characterized as more than merely the biological. In fact, it is portrayed as a textual phenomenon that is plural and disengaged from the contingencies of *a priori* roles: "Nevertheless, once the alternative is rejected (once the paradigm is blurred) utopia begins: meaning and sex become the object of free play, at the heart of which the (polysemic) forms and the (sensual) practices, liberated from the binary prison, will achieve a state of infinite expansion. Thus may be formed a Gongorian text and a happy sexuality" (*RB*, p. 133).

To be sure, the utopia of sexuality evokes a pleasure that refuses to name itself and is situated at the locus of its root-meaning, no-place. The free-play in question here is integral to the quest for an amorphous sexuality: it suggests that it can only have felicitous consequences through an excess of meaning. By equating utopia with the neuter, Barthes opts for a higher form of sexuality reaching beyond social constructions in the name of the transgressive imperatives of desire: "The neuter . . . is a purely qualitative, structural notion; it is what *confuses* meaning, the norm normality. To enjoy the *neuter* is perforce to be disgusted by the *average*" (*SFL*, p. 109).

In a sense, then, the coupling of the erotic and the semiotic in the figure of the neuter produces a radical signifying practice that challenges both closure in gender (i.e., the institution of heterosexuality) and in language. To go beyond the constraints of normality is in fact an attempt to reject the fictional signs of plenitude associated with the quantitative equilibrium of the so-called mythological mean. The abnormal therefore becomes the signifier of the neuter with pleasure defining itself as a form of perversity: "Pleasure is a *neuter* (the most perverse form of the demoniac" (*PT*, p. 65). Perversion becomes an issue because it generates a blissful surplus of meaning, a libidinal flow which frees sexuality from a totalizing homogeneity and allows it to transgress the obstacles of social censure through the active quest for the neuter: "The pleasure potential of a perversion (in that case, that of the two H.'s: homosexuality and hashish) is always underestimated. Law, Science, the *Doxa* refuse to understand that perversion, quite simply, *makes happy* or to be more specific, it produces a *more* . . . and in this *more* is where we find the difference . . ." (*RB*, pp. 63–64).

But this idealized sexuality that Barthes puts forth is suspended somewhere between the satiety of pleasure and its ostensible absence. In a 1979 preface to Renaud Camus's novel *Tricks*, Barthes portrays a utopian erotic rapport as a fiction in which no one player would have a position of dominance over the other. It is, like the imaginary contract of prostitution, an encounter which takes place only once and engages its players in a drama which passes without regret. A trick is indeed more than simply an act of cruising, but it is often infinitely much less than love. It is a metaphor of clandestine adventures that potentially engage the amorous subject in a theatrical event in which the ludic strategies of the players reduce libidinal intensity into surfaces and

sexuality into a form of haiku that permits asceticism and hedonism to coalesce.

In its very essence, then, a trick is a pseudo-affective mode. It
induces a tropistic interaction through a seductive choreographics that absorbs the self into the facticity of illusion. The trick thus
enables the passage from the sexual to the discursive and thereby
becomes a metaphor of mystical experience: "The *Trick* . . . abandons pornography (before having really approached it) and joins
the novel . . . the trick . . . is a virtual love, deliberately stopped
short on each side, by contract a submission to the cultural code
which identifies cruising with Don Juanism" (*RL*, pp. 293–294).
The dramaturgy of the desiring subject transmits an intensity
that is kept in check. Barthes is ostensibly drawn to Camus's narrative by its ability to represent homosexual encounters without
ever directly speaking about them. The narrative allows him to
reflect the essence of the neuter, which is unquestionably an entity without essence beyond the plenitude of being.

It is, however, in *A Lover's Discourse* that Barthes conceptu-
alizes the discourse of love as separate from sexuality, therefore
problematizing the issue of gender once again. Out of the lover's
discourse emerges a persona who is described as being sexually
indifferent and inscribed in a constellation of figures that simu-
late the amorous subject as a feminized being, one who is gender-
marked and experiences a devastating sense of passivity as the
object of desire. Difference is in fact not determined by sexual
identity but rather by the shifting loci of object relations that define a redistribution of power: "Every lover who falls in love at
first sight has something of a Sabine Woman (or of some other
celebrated victim of ravishment) . . . the lover—the one who has
been ravished—is always feminized" (*LD*, pp. 188–189).

Femininity undoubtedly leaves itself open to libidinal colonization; the function of this feminized subject is to be possessed
through a form of domination. The production of a lover's discourse depends to an unsuspected degree on the binding of the
energy of an amorous subject trapped within the entropy of a
male-centered cultural division of gender roles. But if Barthes enables the masculine to become feminine, it is in order to explore
and put into question the association of sexual inversion with
feminization; gender identity is conditioned by the language of
love, which transforms the amorous subject into a transvestite of

sorts whose subversion is realized by the enunciative reversibility
of masculine and feminine: "Any man who utters the other's absence *something feminine* is declared: this man who waits and
who suffers from his waiting is miraculously feminized. A man is
not feminized because he is inverted, but because he is in love"
(*LD*, p. 14).

Falling in love makes the male figure genuinely a man-woman
and inscribes him in the phallocentric plot of female subjection:
"It is their situation in the relation of force that orchestrates some
characters as virile and others as feminine, without concern for
their biological sex" (*OR*, p. 13). In distancing himself from the
anatomy of the gender-marked body, Barthes sets it free in order to
reify the myth of the eternal feminine, which takes the masculine
as its point of origin. Ironically, the subject in quest of the neuter finds himself imprisoned within the parameters of the binary
law: "I must always choose between masculine and feminine,
for the neuter and the dual are forbidden me" ("Inaugural Lecture," p. 460).

Barthes evokes the passivity of the lover only in order to pri-
oritize the primal relationship between the subject and the imaginary (m)other who engenders the birth of desire. In the lover's
discourse, the maternal imago not only becomes the center of the
subject's identity, but it remains an internalized principle of sensuality and corporeal experience whose absence constitutes a
symbolic castration—"seeing oneself abandoned by the mother"
(*LD*, p. 48)—that is indeed the very symptom of this tragically
terminal disease. The absent mother therefore symbolizes a lost
harmony and emblematizes the pain of separation associated
with all love relationships. In a sense, the desired return for the
maternal figure offers the amorous subject renewed hope for symbiotic bliss while at the same time serving to imprison him in the
femininity within himself: "What I expect of the promised presence is an unheard of totality of pleasures, a banquet I rejoice like
the child laughing at the sight of the mother whose mere presence
heralds and signifies a plenitude of satisfactions" (*LD*, p. 119).

Barthes thus stages the lover's discourse as a catastrophic
theatrical event characterized by the nostalgia for a lost maternal
plenitude manifested as the projection of nothingness. The feeling
of abandonment evokes a subject divided between the potential
loss of what can never be recovered and the memory of what can

never be forgotten: "The lover who doesn't forget sometimes dies of excess, exhaustion, and tension of memory . . . as a child, I didn't forget: interminable days, abandoned days when the Mother was working far away I would go, evenings, to wait for her at the U bis bus stop, the Sèvres-Babylone buses would pass one after the other, she wasn't in any of them" (*LD*, pp. 14–15). Like the abandoned child, the lover finds himself in a state of solitude, the consequences of which reveal the inability to complete separation because of a past that cannot be extricated from the present: "I invoke the other's protection, the other's return: let the other appear, take me away, like the mother who comes looking for her child" (*LD*, p. 17). Desire, then, takes the form of a demand addressed to the (m)other who in essence becomes a personification of that very need. Barthes's vocatives are choreographed as a series of fantasies of persecution by a maternal agent of evil who replaces the identical agent of good. The mother is split into contrasting opposites with the menacing object being nothing more than the result of the excessive idealization of the perfect object: "The fade-out of the loved object is the terrifying return of the Wicked Mother, the inexplicable retreat of love, the well-known abandonment of which the Mystics complain . . . I am not destroyed, but dropped here, a reject" (*LD*, p. 113).

But if the bad mother is characterized as one who withdraws her love, the good son refuses to abandon his mother. From the perspective of the amorous subject springs forth the impulse to sustain nurturance and the need to reenact the infant's original pleasures. Quoting the Tao Te Ching, the lover evokes the singularity of his quest to cathect onto the figure of the mother: "I alone am different from other men, / For I seek to suckle at my mother's breast" (*LD*, p. 213). Nurturance is consecrated as an activity by virtue of the Kleinian definition of culture as an effort to repair the damaged world of the Imaginary through the symbolic rediscovery of the mother's body.[11] And it is through the correlation between writing and femininity that the amorous subject is able to compensate for this loss. The scriptural act constitutes itself as a gynotextual activity that elaborates the fiction of absence at the level of the logos and thereby provides the amorous subject with a locus for the projection of the missing object; the wounds of love can be transcended by a discursive performance that bears the marks of the female voice: "Historically, the discourse of absence is carried on by the Woman . . . it is women who give shape to absence, elaborates its fiction, for she has time to do so she weaves and sings . . . the Spinning Songs express both mobility . . . and absence" (*LD*, pp. 13–14).

At the core of the discourse of desire is the rhetoric of the detail. This phenomenon is inextricably linked to the loss of the mother; it functions as a synecdoche that transcends what Barthes terms, in the context of photography, the realm of the *studium* or a culturally coded discourse. Barthes delineates the notion of the *punctum* in *Camera Lucida* as the aspect of the photograph that designates what punctures the *studium* and figuratively injures the spectator, even though he can't articulate precisely why: "A Latin word exists [*punctum*] to designate this wound, this prick, this mark made by a pointed instrument" (*CL*, p. 26). In essence, the *punctum* is that subliminal detail, that "partial object" (*CL*, p. 43), which touches the viewer and unchains a desire reaching a level of orgasmic pleasure and produces a readerly response "at once brief and active" (*CL*, p. 51). This piercing detail, described as both certain and unlocatable, is a vestigial trace of something that is secretly familiar but has undergone repression and exerted a symbolic exercise of force on the desiring subject: "What I can name cannot really prick me. The incapacity to name is a good symptom of disturbance" (*CL*, p. 51). Thus, the power of the detail catalyzes a pathetic struggle to keep memories alive and forestall the death of desire: "Perhaps the *imagination* of detail is what specifically defines Utopia. . . . Detail is fantasmatic and thereby achieves the very pleasure of Desire" (*SFL*, p. 105). In effect, the *punctum* is a tactic of delay that sustains the jubilant reading of a photographic image which surprises by the force of its very presence. "The *punctum*, then, is a kind of subtle *beyond*, as if the image launched desire beyond what it permits us to see . . . always the Photography astonishes me, with an astonishment which endures and receives itself inexhaustibly" (*CL*, pp. 59, 82).

The rhetoric of the detail reaches its most poignant level in Barthes's ruminations on images of the mother in which the son in mourning fetishizes the photographic detail as mediator of desire for the mother and in an effort to master the trauma of her loss. Under the guise of a quest for the essence of photography, the analysis of the image in *Camera Lucida* reveals not only the absent referent common to all photos, but, in addition, the ontological anxiety derived from the Barthesian subject's nostalgia for what has been. "According to these photographs, sometimes I recognized a region of her face, a certain relation of nose and fore-head, the movement of her arms, her hands. I never recognized her except in fragments, which is to say that I missed her *being* and that therefore I missed her altogether. It was not she, and yet it was no one else" (*CL*, pp. 65–66).

Yet this equivocal remembrance enables Barthes to repress even momentarily the pain of separation and to compensate for the loss of a psychic illusion of unity; its stake is undoubtedly in the quest to reconstitute the lost maternal corpus from lacunary fragments and the agony and the ecstasy of that pursuit: "Strain-ing toward the essence of her identity [that of the mother], I was struggling among images partially true, and therefore totally false" (*CL*, p. 66). Barthes's affective investment reveals itself through the hypertrophy of single details that, at best, painfully approximate the image of the maternal body. "The almost: love's dreadful regime, but also the dream's disappointing status . . ." (*CL*, p. 66). They function as a symptom of the need to keep desire alive and resurrect a simulacrum of the absent other through a metonymic process which intermittently allows the part to ex-ceed the whole: "I see, I feel, hence I notice, I observe, and I think" (*CL*, p. 21). The photo thus becomes an allegorical image in which temporality is paradoxically represented as both a triumph and a defeat; it makes a place for a body which, although "hers," had no meaning before this possibility of re-membering.

Fetishism is indeed an issue in *Camera Lucida* because Barthes is caught in an imaginary relationship which nurtures an amorous preference for the mother. This relationship is predi-cated on the denegation of the maternal phallus which serves as a means to avert the threat of his own castration and thereby re-main in an imaginary state of sexual indifference that maintains the Other as the Same.[12] "When I confronted the Winter Garden Photography I gave myself up to the Image . . ." (*CL*, p. 75).[13] Thus, for Barthes the fetishistic attraction to the photographic detail becomes "a model for repudiating reality)."[14] Accordingly, the maternal image carries within it a monument to repression, a spectrum that enables the orphaned spectator to avert the to-tal renunciation of the object of narcissistic desire: "This word [spectre] retains, through its roots, a relation to 'spectacle' and adds to it that rather terrible thing which is there in every photograph: the return of the dead" (*CL*, p. 9). In this context, Barthes's writing puts forth the desire to preserve the unravished purity of illusion in which the filial subject opts for symbiotic dependency with a singular maternal figure.

After his mother's death, the amorous son, while pondering over a photo of her as a child in the Winter Garden scene, uncovers a utopia, the "brighter shadow" (*CL*, p. 116), where wishes are fulfilled.[15] The photo becomes an object of intense affective investment that symbolically consecrates the union of mother and son as the only Nature acceptable to the amorous subject. Yet the moment Barthes sees his mother in the photo he not only attempts to ward off the death he sees inscribed in her girlish picture, but he intercalates it with the story of his own life and the mortality that it implies. The future is imagined from the anticipatory standpoint of its having already occurred and from the consciousness of impending death; unable to think the absence of thought, the Barthesian subject conceives of its mortality through the death and separation from the (m)other. "Once she was dead I no longer had any reason to attune myself to the progress of the superior Life Force (the race, the species). . . . From now on I could no more than await my total, undialectical death" (*CL*, p. 72). As the absence of the mother served as a template for uninterrupted desire in *A Lover's Discourse*, so the death of the mother evoked by the *punctum* of the Winter Garden photography functions as an uncanny harbinger of the death of desire. "For what I have lost is not a Figure (the Mother), but a being and not a being but a quality (a soul): not the indispensable, but the irreplaceable. I could live without the Mother (as we all do, sooner or later) but what life remained would be absolutely and entirely unqualifiable (without quality)" (*CL*, p. 75).

Notes

1. I quote from the following texts: *Writing Degree Zero* (*WDZ*), trans. Annette Lavers and Colin Smith (Boston: Beacon Press, 1970); *On Racine* (*OR*), trans. Richard Howard (New York: Hill and Wang, 1983); *Sade, Fourier Loyola* (*SFL*), trans. Richard Miller (New York: Hill and Wang, 1976); *S/Z* (*S/Z*), trans. R. Miller (New York: Hill and Wang, 1976); *The Pleasure of the Text* (*PT*), trans. R. Miller (New York: Hill and Wang, 1975); *Roland Barthes by Roland Barthes* (*RB*), trans. R. Howard (New

York: Hill and Wang, 1977); *A Lover's Discourse* (*LD*), trans. R. Howard
(New York: Hill and Wang, 1978); "Introduction to the Structural Analy-
sis of Narratives" ("SAR"), in *Image-Music-Text*, trans. Stephen Heath
(New York: Hill and Wang, 1977); "Inaugural Lecture at the Collège de
France" (*L*), in Susan Sontag, ed., *A Barthes Reader* (New York: Hill and
Wang, 1982); *Sollers écrivain* (*SE*) (Paris: Seuil, 1979); *Camera Lucida*,
trans. R. Howard (New York: Hill and Wang, 1981); *The Grain of the Voice*
(*GV*), trans. Linda Coverdale (New York: Hill and Wang, 1985); *The Re-
sponsibility of Forms* (*RF*), trans. R. Howard (New York: Hill and Wang,
1985); *The Rustle of Language* (*RL*), trans. R. Howard (New York: Hill and
Wang, 1986).

2. In "Roland Barthes, sémioclaste?" (*L'Arc* 56 [1974], 17–24),
Françoise Gaillard describes an "eroticism of intelligibility." Upon completion of my essay, I learned that Naomi Schor also discusses the notion
of Barthes's "eroticization of aesthetics" in her *Reading in Detail* (New
York: Methuen, 1987), p. 96.

3. For a more complete analysis of Barthes's anti-Oedipal discourse, see my "Barthesian Freeplay," *Yale French Studies* 66 (1984),
189–210.

4. The study of narrative from a post-Lacanian Oedipal perspective has been undertaken in Robert Con Davis, ed., *The Fictional Father:
Lacanian Readings of the Text* (Amherst: University of Massachusetts
Press, 1981), and Juliet Flower MacCannell, "Oedipus Wrecks," *MLN* 98
(1983), 910–940.

5. Jacques Lacan, *Ecrits* (Paris: Seuil, 1966), p. 115.

6. "[Barthes] uses Nietzsche's methods—the genealogy and the
gay science—to overcome the death drive encountered in his fetishism,
thus transforming a perversion into a technique of critical production"
(Gregory L. Ulmer, "Fetishism in Barthes's Nietzschean Phase," *Papers
on Language and Literature* 14 [1978], 334–355).

7. "Car s'il est chez lui [Barthes] une continuité, c'est bien celle
d'une *intelligence du romanesque* si aiguë, si séduisante qu'elle ne cesse
d'éclipser l'"utopie' plus secrète d'un autre rêve d'écriture qui, depuis les
années d'apprentissage, habite les pages écrites comme le songe d'un
songe" (Philippe Roger, *Roland Barthes, roman* [Paris: Grasset, 1986],
p. 31).

8. See Shirley Nelson Garner, Claire Kahane, and Madelon Spreng-
nether, eds., *The (M)other Tongue: Essays in Feminist Psychoanalytic Interpretation* (Ithaca: Cornell University Press, 1985). Domna Stanton, in
"The Mater of the Text: Barthesian Displacement and Its Limits," *L'Esprit Créateur* 25 (1985), coins the expression "divirilized son."

9. "The discourse of the male weavers rhetorically stages 'woman'
without in any way addressing women" (Nancy K. Miller, "Arachnolo-
gies: The Woman, the Text, the Critic," in N. K. Miller, ed., *The Poetics of
Gender* [New York: Columbia University Press, 1986], p. 271).

10. See Melanie Klein, "The Importance of Symbol-Formation in the Development of the Ego," and "Infantile Anxiety-Situations Reflected in a Work of Art and in the Creative Impulse," in *Love, Guilt, and Reparation and Other Works*, vol. 1 of R. E. Money-Kyrle, ed., *The Writings of Melanie Klein* (London: Hogarth Press, 1975).

11. Klein, "Symbol-Formation," pp. 220, 232.

12. The fetishistic solution is the means to confront and defeat the castration threat. According to Jean Baudrillard, fetishism incorporates the notions of construction, artifice, fabrication, and imitation by signs ("Fétichisme et idéologie: La réduction sémiologique," *Nouvelle Revue Psychanalytique* 2 [1970], 213–226).

13. Barthes writes that the Imaginary may be found "through the Mother, present next to the Mirror" (*RB*, p. 153).

14. Octave Mannoni writes in *Clefs pour l'imaginaire* (Paris: Seuil, 1969) that the fetish becomes the first model of all repudiations of reality.

15. "L'impossible par chance parfois devient possible: comme utopie. C'est bien ce qu'il disait avant sa mort, mais pour lui, de la Photographie du Jardin d'Hiver. Au-delà des analogies 'elle accomplissait pour moi, utopiquement, *la science impossible de l'être unique.*' Il le disait uniquement, tourné vers sa mère et non vers la Mère, mais la singularité poignante ne contredit pas la généralité, elle ne lui interdit pas de valoir comme la loi, elle la flèche seulement, et la signe"; Jacques Derrida, "Les morts de Roland Barthes," *Poétique* 47 (1981), 277. According to Julia Kristeva, "la sélection de Mère [in Barthes] . . . résume *tout*, début et fin condensés" ("La voix de Barthes," *Communications* 36 [1982], 148–149).

MARY LYDON   Amplification: Barthes,
Freud, and Paranoia

---

*It will be understood that I speak of coincidences
and no more.*   —Poe

The disclaimer with which C. Auguste Dupin qualifies his analysis of the mystery of Marie Rogêt imposes itself at the outset of
any attempt to "apply" psychoanalytic principles to the reading
of literary texts. It will be recalled that in the case of the murder
of the beautiful "segar-girl," Dupin neither visits the scene of the
crime nor interviews any of the principals, but bases his analysis
on a comparative study of what Poe calls "the public prints": the
available newspaper accounts of the killing. What makes Dupin's
caveat particularly compelling for the literary critic, therefore, is
that his exposition of the mystery of Marie Rogêt is nothing less
than an *explication de texte*. But this is not all, for Dupin's reading,
ingenious as it is, does not completely solve the mystery. Indeed,
we might say that his reading reveals rather how the mystery
came about, how it constituted itself as mystery, as enigma (from
the Greek *ainnisesthai,* to speak allusively or in riddles). Thus,
Dupin is able plausibly to reconstruct *the manner in which* the
murder was committed, by interpreting the inconsistencies in the

written accounts of the crime. He is even able, by the same means, to deduce how the body of the victim was subsequently disposed of, but he nonetheless remains unable positively to identify the actual murderer, still less to bring him to justice, while his analysis of the motivation for Marie Rogêt's behavior leading up to the crime also remains, of necessity, speculative.

The "public prints" that formed the basis for Dupin's investigation, it may reasonably be assumed, made no overt claim to be read as literature, although the perennially unresolved question "What is literature?" must threaten the legitimacy of even so carefully measured a statement as this. Indeed, the manner in which Poe's story collapses the distinction between literary and "nonliterary" texts is not the least mysterious aspect of "Marie Rogêt." But whether or not self-declared literary texts are constitutionally enigmatic in a way that reporting, be it of an enigma, does not claim to be, it nonetheless behooves the literary critic to approach her material with at least the degree of reticence that Dupin adopts when reading the newspapers. Freud, who was keenly aware of the trap that literature sets for the psychoanalytically inclined reader—a trap into which it is, ironically, the most talented who are most likely to fall—remained constantly sensitive to this point, in contrast to many of his epigones, and thus (appropriately, in the present context) in his brief preface to Marie Bonaparte's *Life and Works of Edgar Poe* he supplies, with characteristic civility, the necessary disclaimer.

"Investigations such as this do not claim to explain creative genius," Freud writes, "but they do reveal the factors which awake it and the sort of subject matter it is destined to choose." With regard to what follows, it will be understood that I unreservedly endorse Freud's statement; indeed, it is one of the guiding principles of the investigation at hand.[1] Beyond that, to paraphrase Dupin, I speak of coincidences and no more.

The "public prints" on which I have chosen to focus (or which have solicited) my attention are chiefly the following: Roland Barthes, *La chambre claire: Note sur la photographie* (1980), *L'Obvie et l'obtus: Essais critiques III* (1982), and *Le bruissement de la langue: Essais critiques IV* (1984); Jacques Derrida, "Les morts de Roland Barthes" (1981); and Freud, "A Case of Paranoia Running Counter to the Psychoanalytical Theory of the Disease" (1915). Since the speculation prompted by these texts must be situated within a larger framework than the limits of this essay afford, and since my stated objective is to reveal the presence of mystery rather than to explain it away, the broader theoretical implications of those coincidences which drew my attention will only be adumbrated here.

It all began for me (but was that really the beginning?) when I happened on a particular passage in *La chambre claire*, a book whose opening sentence—"One day, quite some time ago, *I happened on [je tombai sur]* a photograph of Napoleon's youngest brother, Jerome, taken in 1852" (emphasis added—implicitly evokes coincidence, from *co*, together, and *incidere*, to fall upon or into, to occur, to happen.[2]

In addition to introducing the immediate occasion of *La chambre claire* (appropriately a photograph, given the book's declared subject), this initial sentence, by virtue of the verb *tombai*, and its echo of the tomb (*tombe*), also introduces the virtual focus of the work: death itself. (Ironically, this text, intended as his mother's cenotaph, was destined, as it turned out, to be Barthes's own swan song.) I cite *La chambre claire*, by the way, under its French title throughout, since, exceptionally, given his generally unerring instinct for *le mot juste*—and despite the fact that his choice may be justified by the miniature image of the device reproduced on the front cover of the French edition—Richard Howard's "English" rendering, *Camera Lucida*, leaves something to be desired.[3] Beaumont Newhall, from whose *History of Photography* the cover illustration is taken, provides this brief description of the instrument: "Still another mechanical substitute for artistic skill was the *camera lucida*, invented by the Englishman William Hyde Wollaston in 1806. Drawing paper was laid flat. Over it a glass prism was suspended at eye level by a brass rod. Looking through the prism the operator saw at the same time both the subject and the drawing paper; his pencil was guided by the virtual image."[4]

To the anglophone ear, at least, *camera lucida* has a strictly technical if not (as in Newhall's account) actually pejorative connotation, which the resonance of the vernacular, *chambre claire*, manages to transcend. As Barthes himself remarks elsewhere, Latin, "a juridical and medical language, produces an effect of scientificity (the scientific code)";[5] hence, no doubt, my impression that *camera lucida*, by its very precision, is inadequate to convey the full chromatic range of *la chambre claire*. Just as in "The Mystery of Marie Rogêt," where Dupin's texts are ostensibly English versions of French originals, translation is also at issue here.

The passage that I happened on, hence that happened or, as we say, *occurred* to me (Barthes: "so it seemed that the best word to designate [temporarily] the attraction certain photographs exerted upon me was *advenience* or even *adventure*. This picture advenes, that one doesn't" [pp. 38/19])—the passage that befell me, then, reads thus:

> Ultimately, my objective, what I am seeking in the photo-graph taken of me (the "intention" according to which I look at it) is Death: Death is the *eidos* of that Photograph. Hence, strangely, the only thing that I tolerate, that I like, that is familiar to me, when I am photographed, is the sound of the camera. For me, the Photographer's organ is not his eye (which terrifies me) but his finger: what is linked to the trigger of the lens, to the metallic shifting of the plates (when the camera still has such things). I love these mechanical sounds in an almost voluptuous way, as if, in the Photograph, they were the very thing—and the only thing—to which my desire clings, their abrupt click shattering the deadening overlay of the Pose. For me the noise of Time is not sad: I love bells, clocks, watches and I recall that initially photographic equipment was related to techniques of cabinetmaking and the machinery of precision: cameras, in short, were clocks for seeing, and perhaps in me someone very old still hears in the photo-graphic mechanism the living sound of the wood. (pp. 32–33/14–15; translation modified)

To the ready third ear of what I have called the "psychoana-lytically inclined reader," the echoes in this passage of one of Freud's most hallucinatory case histories, "A Case of Paranoia Running Counter to the Psychoanalytical Theory of the Disease," are resounding;[6] but since all readers' ears may not be so attuned, "the debilitating burden of paraphrase" cannot be avoided.[7] A condensed version of Freud's account of his case would run, there-fore, as follows.

A young woman is brought to Freud's consulting room by the lawyer she has retained to protect her from alleged blackmail by an erstwhile lover. The man, she claims, has had photographs taken of her in a compromising situation and now intends to use these pictures (*Bilder*, p. 234) in order to have her dismissed from her job. The litigant (whom Freud never actually analyzes, as he is careful to point out, though he refers to her as "the patient" [*die Patientin*]) somewhat reluctantly gives him the following account of her situation.

Her suitor, a "highly cultivated" man (*ein sehr gebildeter . . . Mann*, pp. 235/264) to whom she is strongly attracted (though marriage is out of the question, for what Freud calls "external reasons," pp. 235/264), persuades her to visit him in his bachelor quarters during the day. In the course of their lovemaking (which stops short, however, of genital contact) she is startled by a sudden noise, a "kind of knock or tick" (*ein Pochen oder Ticken*, pp. 236/264; translation modified), coming from the direction of a writing desk placed against the window.[8] (The space between desk and window is partially filled by a heavy curtain.) On being asked to account for the noise, her lover casually attributes it to a clock which sometimes, he says, makes such a sound; but when, on her way down the stairs after the assignation, she meets two men whispering conspiratorially and carrying what appears to be a box, she instantly comes to the conclusion (*bildete sie die Kombination*, pp. 236/264) that what they have with them is a camera and that, from a position concealed behind the curtain, they have been photographing her transports. The noise she had heard therefore, so she reasons, is accounted for by the click of the camera's trigger (*das Geräusch des Abdrückens*, pp. 236/264; translation modified).[9]

Freud, initially nonplussed by the apparent absence of homosexuality from the case (against which he would have expected the paranoia to function as a defense), arranges to see the young woman a second time, alone. On this occasion she reveals that she visited her lover not once but twice and that the disruptive noise occurred on the occasion of the second visit. In the interval between the two rendezvous, however, she was upset by the sight of her lover in conversation with an elderly female superintendent at work: a woman who had taken a great liking to her and who reminded her of her own mother. She concluded from their conspiratorial air and what she perceived to be the subsequently altered manner of the superintendent toward her that the man had betrayed her confidence. When accused of this, however, he succeeded in sufficiently "freeing her from her delusion" (pp. 239/ 267) as to persuade her to see him again; but in the wake of the second visit, the persecutory delusion reestablishes itself defini- tively. In the light of this new information, Freud concludes (*bil- dete [er] die Kombination?*) that the alleged noise itself, and not just the theory it inspired, may have been delusional—amount- ing to nothing less than a projection, on the woman's part, of the knocking or beating (throbbing) (*Pochen oder Klopfen*, pp. 244/270) in her clitoris, occasioned by (unresolved) sexual excitement. It is by transforming this sensation into a persecutory act ostensibly orchestrated by the lover, he audaciously argues, that the delu- sion succeeds in preserving intact what he takes to be the young woman's latent homosexual attachment, not to the actual mother (Freud is emphatic on this point) but to the primordial Mother- Image (*zum urzeitlichen Mutterbild*, pp. 240/268) at the expense of the heterosexual relationship whose appeal, though strong, she ultimately resists. Note that it is the delusion which is the agent, in Freud's account, and that it accomplishes its end by "making ingenious use of some accidental circumstances" (*Zufälligkeiten*, pp. 241/268) a word which might equally well be rendered as "coincidences."

The case thus indeed runs counter to the (Freudian) psycho- analytical theory of paranoia, though not, Freud concludes, be- cause there was no homosexual element present, as he had first supposed. In this instance, he reasons, the paranoid delusion had served not as a defense *against* homosexuality, but as a defense *of* it *against* the encroachment of heterosexuality: the former repre- sented by attachment to the primordial Mother-Image, the latter by its eclipse. The insistence of the word *Bild* and its cognates— *Wahnbildung* (delusion), *gebildeter, bildete, Mutterbild*—in Freud's history is, coincidentally, noteworthy, in both the original and the present context, where juxtaposition with *La chambre claire* and its (absent) mother-image brings the imaginary aura of this vo- cabulary into sharper focus.

If this contradictory case (*widersprechenden*, Freud's word, is surely *le mot juste*) is bizarre to the point of straining belief, we might recall that it is the patient's lawyer, a man "experienced enough to recognize the pathological stamp of [her] accusation," who seeks "the opinion of a psychiatrist in the matter" (pp. 263/ 234). Not, banally, because he has already determined that his client is mad, but rather because he has not dismissed the possibility of her being sane (in other words of "her *having* rather than *being*" a case),[10] for the very good reason, he reportedly remarks to Freud, that "what appears to be incredible often actually happens" (pp. 234/263). With that piece of pragmatic legal wisdom firmly in mind, and recalling my declared intention to speak of coincidences and no more, let us turn again to the passage from *La chambre claire* that "originally" (would it have done so had I not already been familiar with Freud's case history?) solicited my attention.

Is it not curious, first of all, that Barthes, who declared "I have a disease, I *see* language,"[11] the writer of such texts as *S/Z*, and the essays on Erté's alphabet and Cy Twombly's singularly graphic art,[12] who consistently privileged the letter throughout his career, should choose to *hear* photography, an intrinsically visual artistic practice—arguably the most uncompromisingly visible language, since it is inscribed by light itself? "Hence, strangely, the only thing that I tolerate, that I like, that is familiar to me, when I am photographed, is the sound of the camera." Note that what Barthes pleasurably hears is the sound of the camera itself in the act of taking a picture, and a picture, furthermore, of himself. And is it not a further coincidence that he should then so readily associate the noise of the camera with the noise of Time, hence with clocks? "For me the noise of Time is not sad: I love bells, clocks, watches. . . . cameras, in short, were clocks for seeing."

Nor is this the only echo of Freud's case history in *La chambre claire*, for in the paragraph immediately before the passage evoking the sound of the camera, and its association with clocks, Barthes, leading up to his theory that Death is the real subject (in every sense) of Photography, expresses anxiety about the uses to which photographs that are taken of one may be put. He describes with considerable feeling how a portrait taken of him by a first-rate woman photographer, a picture that had for once "restored [him] to [him]self" (p. 31), even to capturing the pain of a recent bereavement in his face, was reproduced (distorted beyond recognition by a trick of printing) on the cover of a pamphlet lampooning his language.[13] "I no longer had anything but a horrible disinternalised sinister and repellent face, to match the image that the writers wished to give of my language," he writes

(p. 31), recalling the persecutory nature of Freud's "patient's" delusion, which focuses specifically on photography's invasion of her privacy, and the subsequent malicious use of the images thus obtained.

But the chamber music of *La chambre claire* is not limited to the single note of the sound of the camera, for Barthes identifies the concepts he calls *studium* and *punctum* with the themes of a classical sonata (from the Latin *sonare*, sound, pp. 49/27), and hence photography itself with that musical form. Thus, Derrida, ever alert to the dialectic of sight and sound, is moved to write, reflecting on *La chambre claire* after Barthes's death, "I thought of another connotation of *composition*, as follows: 2) in the ghostly opposition between two concepts, in the S/P, *studium/punctum* duo, composition is music as well. A lengthy chapter might be opened here on Barthes the musician." [14]

Were it to be written, such a chapter would have to trace Barthes's itinerary from "La jeune fille bourgeoise"—the middle-class young lady of *Roland Barthes:*[15] "Surrounded by political upheaval he plays the piano, paints watercolors: all the false occupations of a middle-class young lady in the nineteenth century" (pp. 56/52; translation modified)—through the remarkable essays of the seventies collected, under the rubric "Music's Body," in *L'Obvie et l'obtus* (1982), to the last work, *La chambre claire* (1980). (The dates point to an uncanny aspect of Barthes's literary production: the proliferation of posthumous texts.) But I limit myself here to evoking another of *La chambre claire*'s musical offerings: the subtle counterpoint (*contra punctum*) to the click of the camera's trigger (or shutter) provided by the other pleasurable sound that Barthes singles out for mention, a sound not directly associated with the photographic apparatus, but with his mother and, indirectly, with her image. I mean the click made by the lid of his mother's powder compact "snapping" shut, as English permits us to say: closing, one guesses (in the imagination of the child, at least) on the spectral *Mutterbild* captured in its diminutive mirror. "In order to 'find' my mother, fugitively alas, and without ever being able to hold on to this resurrection for long, I must, much later, discover in several photographs the objects she kept on her dressing table, an ivory powder compact [*poudrier*] (I loved the sound of its lid) . . ." (pp. 101/64; translation modified).

If to give "powder box" for *poudrier* would be to miss this sonority,[16] would it be an overly ingenious use of coincidence (hence delusional) to rediscover in the mother's powder compact the memory trace of *La chambre claire*? Not just the volume (a word whose musical resonance should not be neglected), nor the actual *camera lucida*, the visual device (which functions so enigmatically within it), but the *site*? I mean the *jardin d'hiver*, the setting for the most important photo in Barthes's book: the absent picture of his mother.[17]

Described but not reproduced, hence occupying the center of the volume in a strikingly negative way (*La chambre claire*, in its insistence on the banality of the photograph, exploits the *double entendre* of *cliche:* properly a photographic negative, hence figuratively an overly used expression), this photo represents the mother as a little girl, standing in what Barthes calls *un jardin d'hiver*, a term I would prefer to translate not as "Winter Garden" but as "conservatory": the distinction being significant, to my mind, not so much for the composition of *La chambre claire* as for structuring its reading.[18]

Consultation of *le petit Robert* yields the following definition for *jardin d'hiver:* "pièce vitrée où les plantes sont à l'abri du froid. **V. Serre** [Winter Garden: glassed-in room where plants are protected from the cold. **See Hothouse**]," while pursuit of the reference to *serre* confirms the definition and provides the additional information that *serre* derives from the verb *serrer,* to grip or hold tight—hence the alternative connotation: claw. "**V. Empoigner** [**See Grasp. Grab. Grip**]," we are told, under *serrer,* which brings us, via *poignant* (happily the same in French and in English) to *punctum,* the piercing detail that in certain photographs arrests Barthes's gaze. Pursuit of the signifying chain within which *jardin d'hiver* is inscribed would thus lead to the conclusion that the so-called Winter Garden photograph is literally as well as metaphorically the *point* of *La chambre claire*, or, more accurately, holds the point of the book in reserve. Though appearing, on the face of it, to be utterly disparate, *le jardin d'hiver* and *la chambre claire* (the device) are, one might say, substitutable for each other in Barthes's *imaginaire*, after the manner of the rebuses of dream-imagery, and are hence equipped with all the capacity simultaneously to reveal and conceal that images in the service of what Freud called the dream-work possess. I am suggesting that, mate-

rially speaking, a conservatory, being constructed of glass, is literally a *chambre claire:* that is to say, a *light* room—in direct contrast
to the photographic *dark* room, and hence to the camera's predecessor, the *camera obscura*, which was initially an actual room.[19]

If, as a translation, "conservatory" has the advantage over
"Winter Garden" of being less obscure, as it were, it has the further benefit of referring in English to what the French have called,
since 1789, *le conservatoire*, hence of evoking music and the voice,
that institution having been established specifically to preserve
the musical and dramatic arts. Thus (replicating the counterpoint of the camera lens and the click of the trigger that activates
it), sound and light would coincide in "conservatory" to reflect
the composition of *La chambre claire:* a locution "which no doubt
says more than *camera lucida*," as Derrida percipiently (and,
since he leaves it at that, cryptically) remarks.[20]

Given his notorious penchant for Greek and Latin terms (the
preeminence of *studium* and *punctum* in *La chambre claire* is
characteristic), it is curious that Barthes himself did not choose
the title *Camera Lucida* for his book; particularly since the cover
illustration of the French edition, as I have noted, depicts that
very instrument in use. What seems to me significant is that, in a
notable reversal of his usual tendency, but consistent with the central position the mother occupies in *la chambre claire* (however one
wishes to read that overdetermined expression), Barthes's title is
a translation of the Latin term into the mother tongue. That a
precedent for this uncharacteristic gesture may be found in the
practice of a composer whose music, Barthes writes, "is continually taking refuge in the luminous shadow of the Mother"
lends resonance to my theory that *La chambre claire* is an elaborate spectacle of sound and light:[21] a spectacle ingeniously, if unconsciously, contrived at once to mourn the mother and to stage
whatever conflicting feelings of culpability and fealty her image
may have inspired in her devoted son.[22] The composer in question
is Schumann, whose rendering of traditionally Italian musical
terms in German Barthes singles out for comment in the essay
"Rasch."[23] "The irruption [of words] in the mother tongue in the
musical text is an important phenomenon," he writes (pp. 274/310;
translation modified), declaring furthermore of the seventh *Kreisleriana* that "it knocks, it beats [*ça frappe, ça tape* (p. 265)]" (*pochen, klopfen?*): an echo of Freud's "patient's" auditory delusion

that is nothing short of hallucinatory for any reader familiar with Freud's case who happens upon it.

Claiming that what he hears in Schumann "are blows: I hear what beats in the body, what beats the body, or better: I hear the body that beats" (pp. 265/299), Barthes (in a variation on the sound/image counterpoint we have remarked in *La chambre claire*) insists that this composer's music is "closer to the painted space than to the spoken chain" (pp. 267/301). "Music, in short, at this level," he writes, "is an image, not a language, in that every image, from the rhythmic incisions of pre-history to the frames of comic strips, is radiant [*rayonnant*]" (translation modified). But the beating in Schumann, Barthes continues, "is not a matter of fists beating against the door, in the presumed manner of fate. What is required is that it *beat* inside the body, against the temple, in the sex, in the belly, against the skin from inside, at the level of that whole sensuous emotivity, which we call, both by metonymy and by antiphrasis, the 'heart'. 'To beat' is the very action of the heart . . . but it is also the emblematic word of two languages: linguistics (in the grammatical example '*Peter beats Paul*') and psychoanalysis ('*A child is being beaten*')" (pp. 267/302).

This passage, happily for my purpose, brings the various chords that have been struck here appreciably closer to resolution. (The musical metaphor, besides its appropriateness to the context, is expressly designed to situate my conclusions athwart the logical, as it were, though within the comprehensible: the domain precisely—even to its etymology—of paranoia itself.) The following sentences from "Rasch" may serve to amplify this last point: "It seems then that only Yves Nat and I (if I may say so) hear the formidable end-stops of the seventh Kreisleriana (c). This uncertainty (of reading, of listening) is the very status of the Schumannian text, picked up contradictorily in an excess (that of hallucinated facts) and an evasion (the same text can be played prosaically). Methodologically speaking you might say (or say yet again): the text has no model: not because it is 'free,' but because it is 'different'" (pp. 268/302–303; translation modified).

This "difference," I would add, is not limited to the Schumannian text. As the impossible science of what he calls "a *mathesis singularis*," it haunts all Barthes's interpretations as it does those of every attentive reader and listener. "Am I alone in hearing it?" is the inadmissible question every systematized interpretation is designed to parry.[24] Indeed, it might be argued that an interpretation is systematic precisely in direct proportion to the anxiety of the interpreter in this regard. "The text has no model" leads inevitably to the conclusion that its reading may have none either. When all is said and done, the originality, the liberating influence of Barthes's interpretations come down to this: his willingness to risk proposing a *mathesis singularis* as a critical "method" and, by espousing his own singularity (his oddness), to court folly or at least its reputation.[25] Here a passage at the beginning of *La chambre claire* is illuminating: "It would be better, once and for all, to make a virtue of my protestation of singularity, to try making what Nietzsche called the 'ego's ancient sovereignty' into a heuristic principle. So I resolved to take, as the point of departure for my research, a few photos only: photos that I was sure existed *for me*. Nothing to do with a corpus, a body of work: merely some bodies" (pp. 21/8; translation modified).

"The ego's ancient sovereignty" is, however, as Nietzsche knew and Lacan has shown, delusive, being primordially alienated. This is the basis for Lacan's claim that knowledge (or, perhaps more accurately, cognition) is by its very nature paranoiac. Thus, the mechanism by which what is felt ("what beats," as Barthes would say) in the body is projected onto the image in the mirror stage bears a relation both to the projection of bodily sensation Freud attributes to his *Patientin* and to the auditory delusion Barthes allows he may be subject to when listening to Schumann,[26] the delusion which the essay "Rasch" is designed to articulate, if not to rationalize.

The dilemma of the literary critic, which Barthes addresses (albeit obliquely) in *La chambre claire*, is that what strikes the reader or listener as odd, hence demanding interpretation, may in fact be produced by the oddness, the singularity of the reader herself, may indeed be nothing less than a projection of the situation in which she finds herself. (Viewed from this perspective, by the way, the actual *camera lucida* depicted on the cover of *La chambre claire*, with its capacity to project the image in the artist's eye, assumes a new significance.) But, for the interpretation thus produced to be granted general validity, it is precisely the inaugural projection that must be concealed. What was initially internal to the reader/viewer/listener must eventually come to appear to be internal to the text/image/sound. Coincidence, what occurs to one as odd, is unacceptable as the basis for a systematic interpretation, yet in the absence of such coincidence no interpretation would have been elicited—furthermore, it is by the ingenious use of such accidental circumstances that "rational" explanation is provided and meaning produced.

It is appropriate to invoke the legendary lucidity of paranoiac discourse here, most memorably asserted in Freud's startling pronouncement that "the delusions of paranoiacs have an unpalatable external similarity and internal kinship to the systems of our philosophers."[27] Lacan, however, refines the point in a statement that is particularly helpful to the present discussion. Addressing an audience composed primarily of clinicians on the subject of paranoia, he identifies the difficulty this psychotic state presents with the fact that it is situated precisely within the domain of the comprehensible: "even when what is comprehended cannot even be articulated. . . . It is a matter of things which are already making themselves understood," he says. "And on the strength of this we indeed believe ourselves capable of understanding."[28] But there precisely we are mistaken, Lacan claims, and he proceeds to issue a caveat that may serve as a pendant to the Freudian demurrer with which I began.

Noting that it is inevitably when analysts in training have *understood*, when they are about to close the case with what he calls *une compréhension*, that they must be stopped (since the very confidence of their grasp is a sure indication of their having in fact "botched the interpretation it would have behooved them to make or not to make"), Lacan describes the moment of comprehension as follows: "This usually expresses itself quite naively in the formula—*the subject meant to say that*. How do you know? What is certain is that he did not say it. And more often than not, hearing what he did say, it seems at the very least that a question could have been asked which might perhaps, on its own, have been enough to constitute the valid interpretation, or at least to initiate it" (p. 31).

It has been one of the premises of this essay that *la chambre claire* no doubt says more than *camera lucida*. Listening to Barthes's text as he invites us elsewhere to do ("il y a un *champ d'écoute* du récit écrit" [there is such a thing as the written narrative's *au-*

ditory field]),[29] it has seemed to me that part of what *La chambre claire* gives to understand (without actually articulating it), hence one of its effects, is a certain coincidence of *Muttersprache* and *Mutterbild*, achieved or, more accurately perhaps, adumbrated, by making the metaphorical *camera lucida* literal in the "luminous shadow" of *la chambre claire:* the conservatory of the (absent) mother-image.

But if this missing image (which is described but not reproduced) is the point of Barthes's text, or holds the point in reserve (as I have claimed), it has its counterpart (or counterpoint) in a remarkable image that is conversely reproduced, but not described: the photograph so eloquently placed between Barthes's homage to Sartre's *L'Imaginaire* and his own text.[30]

What strikes the viewer immediately about this, the only color photograph in the volume, the only image, moreover, about which no word beyond its title is uttered, is its intense blue tint and its overpowering eroticism. Is the latter the effect of the darkened room (the antithesis of *la chambre claire*), the swelling pillow directly in front of the curtained window, the V-shaped opening separating the drapes low down, at the pillow's left edge, close, perhaps, to where the potential sleeper/lover's ear might rest? What is the point of this photograph, one is bound to ask, which in the terms established by *La chambre claire* is so deliberately, ostentatiously, pointless (every other photo in the book being captioned by a phrase identifying its *punctum*)? What did Barthes mean to say by this strategically placed image, which is on the one hand prominently displayed and on the other eclipsed by its pendant, the missing image of the mother? Mindful of Lacan's injunction I will not venture an answer, but let the question remain, if not to constitute "the valid interpretation," then "at least to initiate it." Let me, however (pursuing my own associations), recall the curtain that hung between the writing desk and the window in Freud's case history: the space from which the noise (*Geräusch*) was heard,[31] hence the putative site of what might be called paradoxically (echoing the elaborate chiaroscuro of Barthes's text) the candid camera. And let me also cite Barthes's displaced description of this mysterious photograph (for a description, though missing from *La chambre claire*, does exist).

In a text called "Délibération," originally published in *Tel*

Quel in 1979, the year before Barthes's death, and reprinted as the final essay of the posthumous collection *Le bruissement de la langue* (*The Rustle of Language*) in 1984, Barthes, evaluating his attitude toward keeping a journal, reproduces two of his abortive attempts at doing so: one undertaken during his mother's last illness, the other, "more experimental," according to Barthes himself, the account of a single evening, April 25, 1979. It is the latter which concerns us here, and the following passage in particular:

Paris, April 25, 1979

Wasted evening.
. . . .
At the (flaking) Galerie de l'Impasse, I was disappointed: not by D. B.'s photographs (monochromes of windows and blue curtains, taken with a Polaroid camera), but by the frosty atmosphere of the opening. . . . D. S., beautiful and stately, said to me: "Lovely, aren't they?" "Yes, they're lovely" (but it's not much, there aren't enough of them, I added, to myself). All of it was impoverished. And since the older I get, the more courage I have to do what I please, after a second quick tour of the room (I would have gained nothing further by looking any longer), I split and plunged into a futile night on the town, going from bus to bus and cinema to cinema. I was frozen, I thought I had caught bronchitis (I thought of this several times). Finally I warmed myself up a little by having some eggs and a glass of Bordeaux at the Flore, though it was a very bad day: an insipid and arrogant clientèle: no face to become interested in or to fantasize or even make up stories about. The dismal failure of the evening prompted me to try to adopt, finally, the reformed life-style I have been contemplating for so long. Of which this note is the trace.

(Rereading: this extract would give me a definite pleasure because it reawakened the sensations of that evening so vividly; but curiously, what I relived most distinctly, rereading it, was what had not been written, the gaps in what had been noted [la notation]; for example, the greyness of the rue de Rivoli, while I was waiting for the bus, no point in trying to describe it now, by the way, or else I am going to lose it again in favor of another silenced sensation, and

so on ad infinitum, as if resurrection always took place to one side of *the thing said: the place of the Phantom, of the Shadow.)* (pp. 409/368–369; translation modified)

While it would be presumptuous, if not foolhardy, to attempt to fill in the blanks in Barthes's "notation," "the thing said," the signifier, invites the remark that the dramatis personae of this text feature three characters from *La chambre claire:* Barthes, his mother, and Daniel Boudinet, whose initials, as they are sounded in French, so markedly punctuate the enigmatic title: "*Délibéra-tion.*" "Car punctum c'est . . . aussi coup de dés," Barthes writes (*La chambre claire,* p. 49): a phrase that must be cited in French for it to resonate in the present context. ("*Punctum* is . . . also a throw of the dice" unavoidably loses not only the homophony *dé* but the echo of Mallarmé's poem as well.) Lacan, exploiting the *double entendre* of the French verb *entendre* (which means both to hear and to understand), conveys the complexity of what Barthes called "the written narrative's auditory field" with admirable concision: "If there is anything that can introduce us to the dimension of writing as such it is our noticing that the signified has nothing to do with the ears, but only with reading, the reading of what one hears/understands [*entend*] of the signifier. The signified is not what one hears/understands [*entend*]. What one hears/ understands [*entend*] is the signifier. The signified is the effect of the signifier."[32]

"One can go a step further in disproving the accidental nature of the noise," Freud writes, adding, as a prelude to his audacious interpretation, "We do not, however, ask our readers to follow us, since the absence of any deeper analytic investigation makes it impossible in this case to go beyond a certain degree of probability" (p. 270). Inspired by what one might call a personal tick, I have sought to disprove the accidental nature of the noises that punctuate *La chambre claire,* by recourse to a specific instance of the psychoanalytic discourse on paranoia. My objective in doing so has not been to ascribe any clinical disorder to Barthes, still less to determine and articulate what he "meant to say," but rather, following his example and that of Freud, to pursue to its "logical" conclusion my own flash of intuition, my delirium of interpretation: a delirium whose very singularity, I would argue, makes it characteristic of literary criticism, about which it might properly be said (as Freud dared to suggest of philosophy itself) that there is method in its madness.

Notes

1. This holds true even though the texts I am discussing are "critical" rather than "literary," since I hold the distinction to be delusive. On this point, an essay by Michel Butor, "La critique et l'invention," in *Répertoire III* (Paris: Editions de Minuit, 1968), pp. 7–20, trans. Mary Lydon, "Criticism and Invention," *Cream City Review* 8/1–2 (1983), 1–12, is enlightening (and for some readers, perhaps, less rebarbative for being independent of any declared "deconstructive" context).

2. Roland Barthes, *La chambre claire: Note sur la photographie* (Paris: Editions de l'Etoile, Gallimard, Le Seuil, 1980), trans. Richard Howard, *Camera Lucida: Reflections on Photography* (New York: Hill and Wang, 1981).

3. I have consulted Richard Howard's admirable translations wherever they are available. My reading of *La chambre claire* has, however, required that I make some modifications to the English version of this and other texts. All unattributed translations in this essay are my own; whenever texts are cited in their original language and in English, the original page number precedes.

As to *Camera Lucida*, Howard's decision may have been influenced by the prominence of the two Latin terms, *studium* and *punctum*, in *La chambre claire* (chosen, according to Barthes, for lack of precise French equivalents [pp. 48–49]). This would indeed provide a precedent for the Latin title, but though an astute choice, *Camera Lucida* would tend to obscure rather than illuminate the "luminous shadow" of *La chambre claire* as I wish to present it here.

4. *The History of Photography* (New York: Museum of Modern Art, 1949), p. 11.

5. Barthes, "Analyse textuelle d'un conte d'Edgar Poe," in *L'Aventure sémiologique* (Paris: Editions du Seuil, 1985), p. 342. A partial translation of this text by Matthew Ward and Richard Howard has appeared in *On Signs*, ed. Marshall Blonsky (Baltimore: Johns Hopkins University Press, 1985), pp. 84–97.

6. *The Complete Psychological Works of Sigmund Freud*, ed. James Strachey (London: Hogarth Press, 1953), 14:261–273; Freud, *Gesammelte Werke* (London: Imago Publishing, 1946), 10:234–246.

7. The formula is Paul de Man's.

8. Strachey gives "knock or click," obviously anticipating the camera at the expense of the clock, both of which, Freud will argue, are imaginary in any case. It seems appropriate to point out that *Tick* in German also means a quirk, and indeed the *Collins German Dictionary* some-

what facetiously gives the example *Uhren sind sein Tick* (he has a thing about clocks).

9. Strachey gives "shutter," but the verb *abdrücken* refers specifically to the action of squeezing a trigger.

10. The phrase is Naomi Schor's in an essay called "Female Paranoia: The Case for Psychoanalytic Feminist Criticism," *Yale French Studies* 62 (1981), 204–220, reprinted in Schor, *Breaking the Chain: Women, Theory and French Realist Fiction* (New York: Columbia University Press, 1985), which first set me thinking about Poe, Freud, and paranoia. This brilliant essay, though it is to my mind unresolved in a way that curiously replicates "The Mystery of Marie Rogêt," has proved invaluable to me in a variety of contexts: not least on the occasion of my response to Jonathan Culler, "Problems in the 'History' of Contemporary Criticism," at the 1983 meeting of the MMLA (see *Journal of the Midwest Modern Language Association* 17/1 [1984], 3–15). That my response remains unpublished is matter for some (feminist) paranoid delusions of my own.

11. Barthes, *Roland Barthes par Roland Barthes* (Paris: Seuil, 1975), p. 164; trans. Richard Howard, *Barthes by Barthes* (New York: Hill and Wang, 1977), p. 161.

12. "Erté ou A la lettre," "Cy Twombly ou Non multa sed multum," in *L'Obvie et l'obtus* (Paris: Seuil, 1982), trans. Richard Howard, *The Responsibility of Forms* (New York: Hill and Wang, 1985), pp. 99–122/ 103–129 and 145–163/157–177, respectively.

13. The lampoon (*libelle*) in question is Michel-Antoine Burnier and Patrick Rambaud, *Le Roland Barthes sans peine* (Paris: Editions Ballard, 1978). The cover photograph, which is indeed sinister (an effect its lurid orange background does little to diminish), is credited to Sophie Bassouls.

14. Jacques Derrida, "Les morts de Roland Barthes," *Poétique* 47 (1981), 274, reprinted in *Psyché: Inventions de l'autre* (Paris: Editions Galilée, 1987). Steven Ungar's chapter, "Figuration, Musicality, and Discourse," in *Roland Barthes: The Professor of Desire* (Lincoln: University of Nebraska Press, 1983), responds admirably to Derrida's suggestion and has been extremely helpful in the elaboration of the present essay.

15. (Paris: Editions du Seuil, 1975), trans. Richard Howard, *Roland Barthes by Roland Barthes* (New York: Hill and Wang, 1977).

16. *Poudrier* may mean either powder box or compact: Richard Howard opts for the former, whereas my reading inclines me toward the latter.

17. I must note here, parenthetically, that, while verifying the correct use of the term "memory trace," I happened upon the following quotation from Breuer, to whom Freud attributed the thesis that a single apparatus could not perform the functions of perception and memory: "It is impossible for one and the same organ to fulfill these two contradictory conditions. The mirror of a reflecting telescope cannot at the

same time be a photographic plate" ("theoretical" chapter of *Studies on Hysteria* [1895], Standard Edition, 2:188–189 n.). Besides Death and Photography, Memory is a central theme of *La chambre claire*, and the conjunction of the mirror and the photographic plate in Barthes's text uncannily echoes Breuer's image.

18. This reflects Barthes's procedure in his "Textual Analysis of a Tale of Poe": "our aim is not to reconstitute the structure of the text, but to follow the structuration of reading, more important than that of composition (a rhetorical and classical notion)" (p. 86).

19. See Newhall, *History of Photography*, pp. 9–10.

20. Derrida, "Les morts de Roland Barthes," p. 278. It will be remembered that Freud's young woman visited her lover during the day: a fact that would have been essential (given the then state of the art) to the taking of the incriminating photos, hence to her theory, no less than to the (imperfect) fulfillment of the couple's desire. Might it not be suggested, therefore, that the scene of her "crime" (consciously or unconsciously evoked by Barthes's fixation on the sound of the camera) was a *chambre claire*, and by the same token (following Freud's interpretation) also a conservatory for the *Mutterbild*?

21. Barthes, "Aimer Schumann," in *L'Obvie et l'obtus*, pp. 263/298.

22. "Ingeniously *because* unconsciously," perhaps it would be more accurate to say. Recall Freud's comment on the delusion's "ingenious use of some accidental circumstances," quoted above.

23. *L'Obvie et l'obtus*, pp. 265–277/299–312. See the chapter in Ungar referred to above for an illuminating discussion of this essay.

24. "Le grain de la voix," *L'Obvie et l'obtus*, pp. 240/272.

25. On this point, Lacan's discussion of the English word "odd" in his "Séminaire sur la lettre volée," *Ecrits* (Paris: Editions du Seuil, 1966), pp. 11–61, trans. Jeffrey Mehlman in *French Freud: Structural Studies in Psychoanalysis*, Yale French Studies 48 (1972); pp. 39–72, is suggestive.

26. See Lacan, "Le stade du miroir comme formateur de la fonction du Je," in *Ecrits*, pp. 93–100, trans. Alan Sheridan, "The Mirror Stage as Formative of the Function of the I," in *Ecrits: A Selection* (New York: Norton, 1977).

27. Freud, Standard Edition, 17:261.

28. *Le séminaire de Jacques Lacan: Livre III, Les psychoses, 1955–1956* (Paris: Editions du Seuil, 1981), p. 30.

29. "Analyse textuelle," p. 358.

30. The difference between the French and English editions of *La chambre claire* in this regard is significant. Whereas in the French version the photograph is dramatically placed on the recto (what the French call *la bonne page*) of the page immediately following the flyleaf with its inscription: "En hommage à *L'Imaginaire* de Sartre," in the English version it is displaced onto the verso of the page following the table of con-

tents. Whether this was done for economic reasons or out of insensitivity to the *mise-en-pages*, the result is that the effect of the photograph, hence its resonance for Barthes's text, is greatly diminished.

31. The onomatopeia linking *Geräusch, rasch,* and *rascheln* (to rustle) is extremely suggestive for the rustle of Barthes's language. See particularly Barthes's short text on *bruissement* on the back cover of *Le bruissement de la langue.*

32. *Le séminaire, Livre XX, Encore, 1972–1973* (Paris: Editions du Seuil, 1975), p. 34.

STEVEN
UNGAR

Persistence of the Image: Barthes, Photography, and the Resistance to Film

---

It is one thing . . . to apprehend directly an image as image, and another thing to shape ideas regarding the nature of images in general.
—Sartre, *The Imagination* (1936)

The camera gave the moment a posthumous shock, as it were. —Walter Benjamin,
"Some Motifs in Baudelaire" (1939)

The Image as Image

The death of Maurice Merleau-Ponty in 1961 marked a turning point for postwar philosophy in France, ending the intellectual rule of the revised phenomenology that he and his longtime friend, Jean-Paul Sartre, had promoted since translations of Edmund Husserl's and Martin Heidegger's writings first appeared some thirty years earlier. Over the following decade, critiques by Michel Foucault and Jacques Derrida hastened the demise of models of consciousness and of perception going back to Descartes. These critiques—strongly argued and decidedly polemical—entailed their own problems. In particular, their relation to language-based systems growing out of structural linguistics, psychoanalysis, and semiology directed debate away from issues that Merleau-Ponty's death had left unresolved. Roland Barthes's writings illustrate the extent to which such unresolved issues relating to the image resurface in structural analysis and its offshoots. I have chosen to emphasize the image because Barthes's practice of semiology displays an ongoing attention to visual media. Moreover, film and photography continue to serve as test cases for ongoing debates in literary theory as well as in semiology, psychoanalysis, and gender studies.

Barthes's involvement with film is complex to a point where approaches to his writings on the subject are inevitably indirect and synthetic. This is the case, in large part, for two reasons. First, the sum of his writings on film is relatively small and disjointed within his corpus. Moreover, the writings in question range from the theoretical to the anecdotal. One could not seriously entertain a primary identity for Barthes as a film critic or theoretician since no consistent program or doctrine relating to film is discernible. Secondly, Barthes's writings on film derive from a more general involvement with images which should not be misconstrued as abstracted or otherwise removed from parallel inquiries. The point is made succinctly in a fragment of *Roland Barthes:* "On the one hand, what he says about large objects of knowledge (cinema, language, society) is never memorable: the treatise (the article *on* something) is a kind of enormous falling off. Whatever pertinence there happens to be comes only in the margins, the interpolations, the parentheses, *aslant;* it is the subject's voice *off*, as we say, off-camera, off-microphone, offstage."[1]

At first glance, Barthes's writings are unlikely to be seen as pertinent or innovative to film studies *on their own;* that is, without cross-references to the work of specialists. Closer scrutiny belies this impression in regard to texts which directly invoke films or film theory and others which relate to it by extension. In this sense, *Image-Music-Text* is not merely the title of a collection of Barthes's writings selected and translated by Stephen Heath, but evidence of the inevitable insertion of the image into signifying practices ranging from rhetoric to painting and musical performance. In order to understand Barthes's writings on film, we need to make a lengthy detour via the image. So as not to make what follows appear empty exercise, I should state from the start that this detour is not only desirable, but necessary. What begins as a detour comes close to being permanent displacement, so that one might more accurately refer to a resistance to film.

Rigorous definition of the word "image" as graphic or pictorial representation excludes what are commonly referred to as mental, verbal, and perceptual images. We may think we know what we mean when we refer to verbal images, but there are those for whom the expression is meaningful only in a rhetorical or figurative sense.[2] For Barthes, the interplay of word and image is problematized first as the analysis of writings in *Writing Degree Zero* evolves in *Mythologies* into an inventory of rhetorical practices such as advertising ("Soap-powders and Detergents," "Operation Margarine"), photography ("The Face of Garbo"), film ("The Romans in Films"), and spectacle ("The World of Wrestling," "Strip-tease"). As a supplement to the notion of sign in Saussure's 1916 *Course in General Linguistics, Mythologies* provides a double-tiered model of signification which seeks to account for both connotation and denotation. But even when Barthes explores the mythic or ideological discourse underlying an explicit sign of denotation, (as in "Poujade and the Intellectuals" and "African Grammar"), nonverbal meaning—as found in the visual arts and in spectacle—is consistently subsumed within a linguistic model. Barthes's earliest foray into semiology addresses systems of nonverbal meaning without confronting their specificity—that is, without fully accounting for their difference from purely verbal systems.

Barthes's first substantial attempt to deal with the specificity of the image occurs in a 1961 text, "The Photographic Message." For historians of literature and critical theory, the appearance of this text in the inaugural issue of *Communications* marks an initial moment in what Barthes later calls the heroic period of Parisian structuralism. Some five years later, Barthes contributes "Introduction to the Structural Analysis of Narratives" to the eighth issue of the same journal. Along with "Rhetoric of the Image"—which appears in 1964 alongside "The Elements of Semiology" and Metz's "Le Cinéma: Langue ou langage?"—this *Communications* phase of Barthes's involvement with the image carries over an unstable synthesis of phenomenological (or, as Barthes writes, "naïve") descriptions and structural analysis.[3] "The Photographic Message" and "Rhetoric of the Image" extend the major concerns of *Mythologies* in that Barthes approaches the press and advertising photographs as signifying systems grounded in social and historical institutions. At the same time, his reading of the photographic image derives from questions akin to both structural analysis and phenomenology when he considers the image, so to speak, "in itself":

> The emission and the reception of the message both lie within the field of sociology: it is a matter of studying human groups, of defining motives and attitudes, and of trying to link the behavior of these groups to the social totality of which they are part. For the message itself, however, the method is inevitably different: whatever the origin and destination of the message, the photograph is not simply a product or a channel but also an object endowed with a structural autonomy. Without in any way intending to divorce this object from its use, it is necessary to provide for a specific method prior to sociological analysis and which can only be the immanent analysis of the unique structure that a photograph constitutes.[4]

Reflection on the nature of the image points to a concern for object and method of inquiry which Barthes had displaced in *Mythologies* in order to study the historical and social codes essential to all mythic activity. "The Photographic Message" is an attempt to address the image "in itself" without canceling the dynamic model into which—presumably—he wants to reinscribe it. The task is so ambitious that it seems from the start ill-suited to the two-tiered linguistic model of denotation and connotation in whose terms Barthes is able to account for the photographic image only as "*a message without a code*" (*IMT*, p. 17). The formulation is notorious, infelicitous to a point where Barthes modifies it in a number of texts until he more or less retracts it some twenty years later when, in *Camera Lucida*, he writes that the question of whether or not photography is analogical makes for the wrong approach: "The realists, of whom I am one and of whom I was already one when I asserted that the Photograph was an image without code—even if, obviously, certain codes do inflect our reading of it—the realists do not take the photograph for a 'copy' of reality, but for an emanation of *past reality:* a *magic,* not an art."[5] After the fact, Barthes recognizes the problem even though, at the time, he persisted in approaching the image as a discrete entity—that is, as though it could be detached from function and context.

"Rhetoric of the Image" addresses the implications of approaching the image as an analogical language. Thus, Barthes argues, linguists often refer to the poverty of the image, as though it were a weak (or alternately strong) signifying system: either rudimentary in comparison with language or somehow rich and inexhaustible in its ineffability. Elsewhere in the same text, Barthes counters allegations of the image's intrinsic poverty. He argues that its polysemous nature has been perceived historically as an excess which must be reduced to determinate and stable form: "Polysemy poses a question of meaning and this question always comes through as a dysfunction. . . . Hence in every society various techniques are developed, intended to *fix* the floating chain of signifiers in such a way as to counter the terror of uncertain signs; the linguistic sign is one of these techniques" (*IMT*, p. 39). Not only does Barthes here assert the irreducible difference of the image, but he also accounts for that difference when he relates it to the anchorage and relay functions in the text of the press photograph.

Barthes's inscription of word and image within a relay-text invokes for the first time the element of movement (the kinematics) that announces a progression beyond the static image: "While rare in the fixed image, this relay-text becomes very important in the film, where dialogue functions not simply as elucidation but really does advance the action by setting out, in the sequence of the messages, meanings that are not found in the image itself" (*IMT*, p. 41). "Rhetoric of the Image" marks the breakup of Barthes's early engagement with phenomenology—that is, of his attempts to approach the image as a thing-in-itself. The displacement has both long-term and immediate consequences. First, it recasts what Barthes had formerly referred to as the uncoded analogue within an inquiry into reference which, while unresolved, receives full expression in the sections of *Camera Lucida* dealing with the photographic referent. More immediately, Barthes seems ready to adapt the linguistic model to the very kinds of figurative "languages" disparaged by traditional linguists and philosophers.

The notion of relay-text has direct bearing on film studies and on the theory of film. An immediate difference in vocabulary replaces the former terms of message and communication with text and signification. In fact, Barthes's model remains two-tiered: the relay-text is a construct of relations between word and image corresponding in large part to movement along the vertical axis

of signification and the Saussurean emphasis on *langue* as entity
or system. But a fuller dynamic model of signification would also
entail a supplement of this model by the horizontal axis to account for the temporal sequence of individual utterances with a
resulting emphasis on movement and duration. For students of
film, the coordination of the paradigmatic and syntagmatic axes
has strong associations with the notion of montage in the writings of S. M. Eisenstein and, in particular, with the problems inherent in moving *beyond* the image and *toward* film. It is this very
problematic which Bathes confronts in his 1970 text, "The Third
Meaning: Research Notes on Some Eisenstein Stills."

A decade after "The Photographic Message," the picture has—
so to speak—changed. The visual arts figure directly in the expanded notion of semiology visible in *S/Z*, *The Empire of Signs*,
and *Erté*, all of which appear in 1970. In "The Third Meaning,"
Barthes recasts denotation and connotation as informational and
symbolic levels of meaning. To these, he adds an element which
at first he describes only in its immediacy: "I read, I receive (and
probably even first and foremost) a third meaning—evident, er-
ratic, obstinate. . . . I am not sure if the reading of this third
meaning is justified—if it can be generalized—but already it
seems to me that its signifier (the traits to which I have tried to
give words) possesses a theoretical individuality" (*IMT*, p. 53).
For Barthes, the third meaning is initially perceived as a disruptive excess: "the 'one too many,' the supplement that my intellec-
tion cannot succeed in absorbing" (*IMT*, p. 54). Not merely removed from communication and signification but also a difference
internal to them, the third meaning has a number of functions.

First, it is a provisional limit or border on the basis of which
Barthes differentiates obvious from obtuse processes: "In other
words, the obtuse meaning is not situated structurally, a seman-
tologist would not agree as to its objective existence (but then
what is an objective reading?)" (*IMT*, p. 60). Moreover, the Eisenstein stills illustrate what Barthes terms the filmic as that in film
which is both within and beyond language:

> The filmic, then, lies precisely here, in the region where
> articulated language is no longer more than approximative
> and where another language begins (whose science, there-
> fore, cannot be a linguistics, soon discarded like a booster

rocket). . . . Forced to develop in a civilization of the signified, it is not surprising that (despite the incalculable
number of films in the world) the filmic should still be
rare (a few flashes in SME, perhaps elsewhere?), so much
so that it could be said that as yet the film does not exist
(any more than does the text); there is only "cinema," language, narrative, poetry, sometimes extremely "modern,"
"translated" into "images" said to be "animated." Nor
is it surprising that the filmic can only be located after
having—analytically—gone across the "essential," the
"depth," and the "complexity" of the cinematic work; all
those riches which are merely those of articulated language, with which we constitute the work and believe we
exhaust it. The filmic is not the same as the film, is as far
removed from the film as the novelistic is from the novel.
(*IMT*, p. 65)

The filmic is not simply other than the film. In the functions
and ambitions that Barthes confers on it, the filmic relates to film
as a process of meaning much in the way that *S/Z* asserts structural analysis via an excessive demonstration that is ultimately
subversive. More to the point, the filmic seems to stop short of the
cinematic by invoking the practice of montage, which commonly
exemplifies meaning in the cinema as a coordination of paradigmatic and syntagmatic axes. The gesture on Barthes's part is
openly ambivalent and thus of particular interest as an act of resistance. Where Eisenstein argues for a synthesis in which individual shots are inscribed within a sequence to form a meaningful combination, Barthes willfully stops at the still and thereby
removes the concept of montage from its original context. The result demonstrates the very kind of subversion which the obtuse
third meaning operates on the obvious discourses of information
and signification.[6]

Barthes's revised version of Eisenstein's montage is in line
with the self-conscious elaboration of his critical practice from
S/Z through *Camera Lucida*. In "The Third Meaning," the gesture
already takes the form of a primal scene of recognition such as
those staged later in *The Pleasure of the Text* and *A Lover's Discourse*. From the critical object of the Eisenstein stills, Barthes
moves toward the critical subject in order to consider what moti-

vates its particular stake or position: "I at first ascribed this taste for stills to my lack of cinematic culture, to my resistance to film" (*IMT*, p. 66). Such resistance should not be confused with simple negation. Instead, it asserts the specific value or essence of the filmic in a signifying process which neither photography nor painting fulfills since they lack the possibility of configuration which Barthes associates with diegesis. The relevant point is that Barthes sees this configuration as distinct from the illusion of animated representation in traditional film theory such as that of montage. What Barthes explores in the Eisenstein stills is not their potential function within sequence and montage, but something on the order of a second text (palimpsest or hieroglyph) whose existence never exceeds the fragment: "The still offers us the *inside* of the fragment. In this connection we would need to take up—displacing them—Eisenstein's own formulations when envisaging the new possibilities of audio-visual montage: the basic center of gravity . . . is transferred to *inside* the fragment, into the elements included in the image itself. *And the center of gravity is no longer the element 'between shots'—the shock—but the element 'inside the shot'—the accentuation within the fragment"* (*IMT*, p. 67).

To summarize at this point, Barthes's writings on the image during the 1960s are seemingly blocked at a notion of the filmic which he openly distinguishes from film. Barthes never really follows through on the program outlined in "Elements of Semiology" because his own concerns shift to a point where that model no longer corresponds to his revised notions of figuration and text. After "The Third Meaning," a final set of writings elaborates an ambivalence which, I believe, should be understood as nothing less than a resistance to the cinema. It is that resistance—and its meaning—which Barthes addresses in three of his last writings: *The Pleasure of the Text, Roland Barthes,* and *Camera Lucida.*

The Image as Point of Death and Sexuality

Eisenstein's writings emphasize the dynamics of sequential exposition corresponding to the syntagmatic axis of signification. Montage occurs on the basis of what Eisenstein refers to as an integral image whose emergence concretizes a maximum of emotion and power. The key term of emergence marks an aesthetic experience in which creator and consumer participate actively:

> Every spectator, in correspondence with his individuality, and in his own way and out of his own experience—out of the womb of his fantasy, out of the warp and weft of his associations, all conditioned by the premises of his character, habits and social appurtenances, creates an image in accordance with the representational guidance suggested by the author, leading him to understanding and experience of the author's theme. This is the same image that was planned and created by the author, but this image is at the same time created also by the spectator himself.[7]

This passage is close to prophetic; one might easily mistake it for Barthes's account of the dynamics of reading and the binary of readerly and writerly texts in S/Z. It also recalls *The Pleasure of the Text* and a theory of the text as perpetual working and reworking of a generative idea, with a loss or unmaking of the subject in Barthes's notion which has no apparent equivalence in Eisenstein's theory of montage.

The primacy of the aesthetic experience for both Eisenstein and Barthes points to a common concern for representation. In "Word and Image," Eisenstein describes representation as a documentary function producing affidavit-expositions "shot from a single set-up." Against these, he asserts the singular virtue of montage construction fashioned by artists: "that great power of inner creative excitement in the *spectator* which distinguishes an emotionally exciting work from one that stops without going further than giving information or recording events" (*The Film Sense*, p. 35). In *The Pleasure of the Text*, Barthes sets representation against figuration, casting the former negatively as encumbered with meanings other than that of desire. To illustrate this difference, he refers at length to a text by Barbey d'Aurevilly and concludes as follows: "That is what representation is: when nothing emerges, when nothing leaps [*quand rien ne sort, rien ne saute*] out of the frame: of the picture, the book, the screen" (*Pleasure*, p. 57). Against representation, figuration becomes an appearance of the erotic body, leading to a text split into fetish objects. Ultimately, the felicitous or privileged form of figuration mixes word and image: "Similarly, and even more than the text, the film will *always* be figurative (which is why films are still worth making)— even if it represents nothing" (*Pleasure*, p. 56).

Midway through *The Pleasure of the Text*, Barthes describes the asocial character of bliss (*jouissance*) in terms which suggest that solitude, separation, and loss are the inevitable price of surrender to overwhelming sensation: "*Everything* is lost, integrally. Extremity of the clandestine, darkness of the motion-picture theater" (*Pleasure*, p. 39). The statement expresses a radical hedonism, almost as though Barthes were taking Susan Sontag at her word when—a decade earlier, in *Against Interpretation*—she called for an erotics of art. Nevertheless, Barthes remains enough of a structuralist by habit to set any willful attempt to lose the self within an overriding project of observation. As a result, resistance always keeps *jouissance* partial; the critical subject returns, if only in fragments. If Barthes confesses to deriving intense pleasure from (and *within*) the darkness of the motion-picture theater, he still comes back out—so to speak—into the broad daylight of the "real world."[8]

In *Roland Barthes*, the interplay of pleasure and resistance is reasserted even more openly: "Resistance to the cinema: the signifier itself is always, by nature, continuous here, whatever the rhetoric of frames and shots; without remission, a continuum of images; the film (our French word for it, *pellicule*, is highly appropriate: a skin without puncture or perforation) *follows*, like a garrulous ribbon: statutory impossibility of the fragment, of the haiku" (*Roland Barthes*, pp. 54–55). But no sooner does Barthes acknowledge the force of the cinematic signifier than he identifies certain compromising constraints of representation that make it somehow insufficient. Elsewhere in the same text, Barthes asserts the pleasure of the theater against cinema and painting. Of all the figurative arts, theater alone presents bodies and not their representation: "The cinema would be like those bodies which pass by, in summer, with shirts unbuttoned to the waist: *Look but don't touch*, say these bodies and the cinema, both of them, literally, factitious" (*Roland Barthes*, p. 84). The reference to theater sets Barthes's resistance to film within traditional aesthetics and the problematics of correspondence and/or specificity among the arts. It also points to revised notions of figuration and textuality as a staging which both establishes and disperses the subject. As

Barthes puts it in *The Pleasure of the Text*, the primary emphasis is on process rather than product: "The generative idea that the text is made, is worked out in a perpetual interweaving; lost in this tissue—this texture—the subject unmakes himself, like a spider dissolving in the constructive secretions of its web" (*Pleasure*, p. 64).

By the time *Camera Lucida* appears in 1980, the film image is definitively mediated by Barthes's involvement with photography. At first glance, this last book regresses to a methodology of some twenty years earlier as Barthes invokes a phenomenological idiom revised via structural analysis. Thus, he states that he wants to find out what photography is "in itself" and that he prefers photography *in opposition to* the cinema (*la Photo contre le cinéma*). The convergence of value and analysis leads Barthes to recognize the inadequacy of his earlier approaches: "*Affect;* affect was what I didn't want to reduce; being irreducible, it was thereby what I wanted, what I ought to reduce the Photograph *to;* but could I retain an affective intentionality, a view of the object which was immediately steeped in desire, repulsion, nostalgia, euphoria?" (*Camera Lucida*, p. 21).

Once he considers the element of affect, Barthes must also contend with the inherent tautology of the photo that seemingly coincides with its referent: "The Photograph belongs to that class of laminated objects whose two leaves cannot be separated without destroying them both" (*Camera Lucida*, p. 6). This adherence of the referent should not, however, be confused with representation in a conventional sense. For what Barthes comes to see as the affective intentionality drawing him toward the photo is the detail (or *punctum*) whose emergence invariably supplements the informational or symbolic meaning. Thus, where the term "reference" commonly designates a relation to something outside language (something "out there" or "in the real world"), Barthes makes text and image the means of staging a personal drama:

> I call "photographic referent" not the *optionally* real thing
> to which an image or a sign refers but the *necessarily* real
> thing which has been placed before the lens, without
> which there would be no photograph. Painting can feign
> reality without having seen it. Discourse combines signs
> which have referents, of course, but these referents can be

and are most often "chimeras." Contrary to these imitations, in Photography I can never deny that *the thing has been there*. There is a superimposition here: of reality and of the past. And since this constraint exists only for Photography, we must consider it, by reduction, at the very essence, the *noeme* of Photography. What I intentionalize in a photograph (we are not yet speaking of film) is neither Art nor Communication, it is Reference, which is the founding order of Photography. (*Camera Lucida*, pp. 76–77)

This personalized meaning of the term "reference" allows us to understand the affective essence which Barthes seeks throughout *Camera Lucida* through comparisons of painting and theater to film. At one point, Barthes compares certain photographs to the paintings by Jean-Baptiste Greuze which stage moralistic scenes within a single tableau. Elsewhere, he asserts that photography touches art not by painting, but by the theater: "The *camera obscura*, in short, has generated at one and the same time perspective painting, photography, and the diorama, which are all three arts of the stage" (*Camera Lucida*, p. 31). For Barthes, the text mediates between a referent in the common sense of something "outside" or "beyond" language and a more personal drama whose movement generates the staging referred to above as figuration. For Barthes, this staging can occur in various media and genres, especially when the specificity of material and form is sacrificed in favor of affective power.

The resistance to film asserted in *Camera Lucida* is already present in a 1973 text, "Diderot, Brecht, Eisenstein," in which theater, painting, cinema, and literature are classified as *dioptric arts:* "The tableau (pictorial, theatrical, literary) is a pure cut-out segment with clearly defined edges, irreversible and incorruptible; everything that surrounds it is banished into nothingness, remains unnamed, while everything that it admits within its field is promoted into essence, into light, into view" (*IMT*, p. 70). Using Diderot as his major point of reference, Barthes characterizes a fetishism of the image based on a dramatic unity such as that which desire and mourning impose on his reading of the Winter Garden photo in *Camera Lucida*. In the 1973 text, Barthes describes how such dramatic unity is conveyed in film. Once again, the example invoked is that of Eisenstein:

The film is a continguity of episodes, each one absolutely meaningful, aesthetically perfect, and the result is a cinema whose vocation is anthological, holding out to the fetishist, on dotted lines, the fragment to be cut out and taken away to enjoy. (Isn't it said that in some *cinémathèque* or other a piece of film is missing from the copy of *Potemkin*—the baby carriage scene, of course—snipped and stolen by some film lover as if it were a lock of a woman's hair, her glove or her underwear?) This is Eisenstein's primacy power: no *single image is boring*, we are not forced to wait for the next one in order to understand and be delighted: no dialectic (that interval of patience necessary for certain pleasures), but a continuous jubilation, consisting of a summation of perfect moments.[9]

Eisenstein's notion of montage evolves over the better part of twenty years, but the basic problematic of relating frame and sequence remains a constant. Like Barthes, Eisenstein wants to determine the specificity or essence of film and winds up instead with a limited correspondence among the arts. In *Camera Lucida*, the fetish of the photo image is symptomatic of an affective intensity whose referent is the personal drama of death foretold (foreseen?) in the Winter Garden portrait of Barthes's mother as a girl. *Camera Lucida* suggests that Barthes's assertion of the photographic image in opposition to film grows out of a deeper sense of interaction based less on film than on theater. To put this another way, spectator positioning in film is passive to a degree which seemingly precludes intervention. Motion pictures stage an inevitable passage toward completion which theater slows: one could conceivably jump onto the stage and "stop the show." Photography freezes that passage via compression within a single frame: "Photography is a kind of primitive theater, a kind of *Tableau vivant*, a figuration of the motionless and made-up face beneath which we see the dead" (*Camera Lucida*, p. 32).

The opposition between photography and film marks a limit of Barthes's semiology. It also asserts what André Bazin describes in 1945 as the mummy complex, in terms of which Barthes's primal theater of photography expresses a desire to maintain the appearance of life in the face of death: "To preserve, artificially, his bodily appearance is to snatch it from the flow of time, to stow it away neatly, so to speak, in the hold of life."[10] The priority of the photograph's psychological function—the "instrumentality of a non-living agent"—corresponds to the impact of the *punctum* that Barthes describes some thirty-five years later. In fact, the following passage by Bazin might easily be mistaken as coming from *Camera Lucida:* "Hence the charm of family albums. Those gray or sepia shadows, phantomlike and almost undecipherable, are no longer traditional family portraits but rather the disturbing presence of lives halted at a set moment in their duration, freed from their destiny; not, however, by the prestige of art but by the power of an impressive mechanical process: for photography does not create eternity, as art does, it embalms it, rescuing it simply from its proper corruption" (Bazin, p. 14).

Camera Lucida's complexity complicates any attempt to see it as a definitive statement of Barthes's involvement with film. Where Eisenstein constructs montage on the basis of the minimal unit of the shot, Barthes's analysis is ill-suited for rigorous application because the movement that draws him to the image is affective rather than cinematic. Even the phenomenon of framing holds less promise for the study of film than as a means of approaching what he calls the filmic or "third" meaning. Ultimately, Barthes's relation to film is tied to his attempts to articulate the interplay between deep and surface phenomena. This is why the phenomenology invoked in *Camera Lucida* is less of a simple regression than a critical return to problems of perception via psychoanalysis and semiotics. This is also to say that the direct application of Barthes's writings on film to practical analysis is ill-advised without adjustment, because the dynamic of representation drawing him to the image derives from the theater as well as from modes such as the *tableau vivant* and *diorama*.[11] In *Camera Lucida*, the photograph objectifies affect and a momentary stoppage of time responding to a personal imperative. For Barthes, this singular capacity sets the photograph apart from the motion picture, allowing for a persistence of the image which film never achieves.

Subjected to the Image

What, then, is the image *for Barthes* and what might his resistance to film add to our understanding of his writings on the sign?

Some closing remarks in the guise of a conclusion. First, an over-view of Barthes's evolving views on the image corrects the mis-conception that the phenomenological idiom in *Camera Lucida* marks a direct and uncritical regression from the semiology that had seemingly displaced it some twenty years earlier. In fact, the relation of phenomenology to semiology within Barthes's writ-ings does not lend itself to a simple and neat progression. The semiotics of the image developed over the *Communications* phase of the 1960s is neither negated nor otherwise phased out in *Cam-era Lucida*. Instead, Barthes's book-length note on photography is the last in a series of illustrations that meaning is inevitably grounded or located in a specific time and place and that un-limited semiosis is possible only in theoretical terms. The point is first made in *Mythologies,* where the denotation that Barthes re-ferred to as "the mythic activity" is studied in the ways that ad-vertising and popular press photographs illustrate capitalism and a colonialist mentality, respectively. Where the study of the image in *Mythologies* is carried out in social and economic terms, *Camera Lucida* is also a narrative of mourning whose ties to death and sexuality lend themselves to the more primal insight af-forded by psychoanalysis.

"The Third Meaning" significantly revises Barthes's semiot-ics of the image from the social categories of *Mythologies* toward the intimate family drama of *Camera Lucida*. First and foremost, it invents the still image by excising it from the film strip. As a result, the photo derived from film inverts the customary progres-sion from still to moving image, as though the former somehow contained—in a compressed and frozen state—the energy and movement of the latter. The figurative violence that produces the Eisenstein still acquires a different function in *Camera Lucida,* where the Winter Garden photograph operates a stoppage of time that is openly artificial. The photo of the mother as child serves as a fiction of convenience that momentarily eases the emotion of mourning. The progression from "The Third Meaning" to *Camera Lucida* ends with a conception of the image that borders on the fetishistic. (Barthes uses the very term in the passage from "Di-derot, Brecht, Eisenstein" quoted above.)

Even more suggestive is a second question raised by "The Third Meaning": the status to be granted to this progression. To restate this another way, we might echo Naomi Schor's concern for determining what aesthetic system, if any at all, is implied by Barthes's aesthetic practice.[12] Victor Burgin goes even further by projecting through what he sees as Barthes's untheorized observations on the image the necessity for a "psychopathology of everyday representation" based on a type of relation between movie and still images.[13]

The comments by Schor and Burgin help us to inscribe the last phase of Barthes's writings on photography and film within his evolving practice of semiology. Clearly, the notion of a systematic aesthetics (or aesthetic system) is made dubious by the fact that Barthes's death weakens any attempt to impose closure on a progression that remains interrupted and incomplete. Moreover, what Schor describes as Barthes's detotalized and fragmentary aesthetics is already so evident within the individual texts starting with "The Photographic Message" that rigorous systematicity is simply ill-conceived. More promising and more suited to the discontinuity noted above is the sense that Barthes's writings on the image resist or are otherwise incommensurate with systematicity. (An alternative formulation would be that they illustrate or dramatize this incommensurability before—if ever at all— they theorize.) Schor contrasts the detotalized and fragmentary elements of Barthes's writings to the systematized totalizing elements in Hegel's aesthetics. Moreover, she sets Barthes against Hegel in terms of what she refers to as the modernist project of restoring realist details to their "brute and unsublimated materiality" (Schor, p. 84).

What Schor refers to as the work of *desublimation* also valorizes the priority of illustration over abstraction. In textual terms, Barthes's writings on the image internalize what others might designate as theory. His semiotics of the image evolves toward a dynamic of figuration that is increasingly personal. The progression that ends with the Winter Garden photo in *Camera Lucida* begins with the Eisenstein still as fetish in "The Third Meaning" and continues with the representative fragment in "Diderot, Brecht, Eisenstein."

Notably, the latter text adds the concept of the *tableau* (both painting and fragment) as intermediary form of representation between film and photo. Barthes invokes Lessing's "pregnant moment" to extend a classical notion of turning point (*peripateia*) that the late Henri Cartier-Bresson revises in the title of his

1952 collection of photographs, *The Decisive Moment* (Burgin, pp. 89–90) and that is also resonant with Eisenstein's notion of the integral image. The conflation of terms and modes of representation from "The Third Meaning" to *Camera Lucida* extends Barthes's valorization of the photograph's singular capacity to objectify emotion and meaning within time. The photographic *mise-en-scène* may well imply a theoretical position and a hierarchy among various modes of representation. But any such theorization is secondary to the illustration of photography's specificity and irreducible difference from painting and film. From message to *punctum*, Barthes's involvement with the image also illustrates with disarming simplicity the strong affective motivation within what might otherwise be taken for an abstract and/or disinterested inquiry.[14]

Notes

1. Roland Barthes, *Roland Barthes*, trans. Richard Howard (New York: Hill and Wang, 1977), p. 73.

2. This definition, set forth by P. N. Furback in *Reflections on the Word "Image,"* is discussed by W. J. T. Mitchell in *Iconology: Text, Image, Ideology* (Chicago: University of Chicago Press, 1986), pp. 11–13.

3. This specific series of articles is completed when Barthes contributes "En sortant du cinéma" (Leaving the Movie Theater) to *Communications* no. 23, a special issue on "Psychoanalysis and Cinema" edited by Raymond Bellour, Thierry Kuntzel, and Christian Metz. A translation of Barthes's text appears in *The Rustle of Language*, trans. Richard Howard (New York: Hill and Wang, 1986).

4. Barthes, "The Photographic Message," in *Image, Music Text*, trans. Stephen Heath (New York: Hill and Wang, 1977), p. 15. Future references cite this collection as *IMT*.

5. *Camera Lucida: Reflections on Photography*, trans. R. Howard (New York: Hill and Wang, 1981), pp. 88–89. Three years after "The Photographic Message" and in the name of structuralist film theory, Christian Metz appropriates the notion of the photograph as a message without out a code when he refers to film as a language (*langue*) without a code. See Paul Sandro's cogent overview of and commentary on Metz's early film theory, in "Signification in the Cinema," reprinted in Bill Nichols, ed., *Movies and Methods* (Berkeley: University of California Press, 1985), 2: 391–407.

6. Metz distinguishes between film and cinema in order to account for the former's specificity. Where the word "film" refers to the material object in the real world, "cinematic" designates an abstraction made up

of multiple systems. See Sandro, "Signification in the Cinema," pp. 393–394, and Stephen Heath, "Metz's Semiology: A Glossary," *Screen* 14/1–2 (Spring–Summer 1973): 214–226.

7. Sergei M. Eisenstein, "Word and Image," in *The Film Sense*, trans. Jay Leyda (New York: Harcourt Brace Jovanovich, 1975), p. 33.

8. This entering and leaving is the very gesture of ambivalence that Barthes evokes in "Leaving the Movie Theater."

9. "Diderot, Brecht, Eisenstein," in *IMT*, pp. 72–73. I have mixed Heath's translation with some of Richard Howard's felicitous phrasing from his translation of the same text, in *The Responsibility of Forms* (New York: Hill and Wang, 1985).

10. André Bazin, "The Ontology of the Photographic Image," in *What Is Cinema?*, trans. Hugh Gray (Berkeley: University of California Press, 1970), p. 9. Elsewhere in *Camera Lucida*, Barthes invokes Bazin's notion of the blind field of the cinematic screen. Yet once Barthes perceives the *punctum* of the photographic referent, even the still photo creates its own blind field, allowing for the *emergence* which he and Eisenstein both deem essential to the aesthetic experience. Behind (or within) the visible image, then, what Barthes terms the *punctum* "brings out" the essential image, the other stage of personal drama. (I am grateful to Brian Duren for directing me to the Bazin article.)

11. Walter Benjamin's discussion of experience, shock, and sensation in "Some Motifs in Baudelaire," in *Illuminations*, trans. Harry Zohn (New York: Schocken, 1969), is characteristically prophetic, reiterating Baudelaire's doubts in "Le public moderne et la photographie" (1859) as well as his own views developed at length in "The Work of Art in the Age of Mechanical Reproduction," in *Illuminations*, pp. 217–252.

12. Naomi Schor, "Desublimation: Roland Barthes's Aesthetics," in *Reading in Detail: Aesthetics and the Feminine* (New York: Methuen, 1987), p. 80.

13. Victor Burgin, "Diderot, Barthes, *Vertigo*," in Victor Burgin, James Donald, and Cora Caplan, eds., *Formations of Fantasy* (New York: Methuen, 1986), p. 86.

14. A short version of this essay was first given in April 1986 for a session of the proseminar on theory in the Department of Romance Studies at Cornell University. I thank David Grossvogel and Philip Lewis for their interest, criticisms, and encouragement in this instance and in the past.

Contributors

ANTOINE COMPAGNON, professor of French at Columbia University, is editor of *Prétexte: Roland Barthes* (1978) and author of essays and novels including *La seconde main ou le travail de la citation* (1979), *Le deuil antérieur* (1979), *Nous, Michel de Montaigne* (1980), and *La Troisième République des lettres* (1983). He has recently contributed to the new four-volume edition of Proust's *A la recherche du temps perdu* published in the Bibliothèque de la Pléiade.

RICHARD HOWARD is a Pulitzer Prize–winning poet and writer who has translated almost all of Barthes's major works as well as novels by André Gide, Alain Robbe-Grillet, and Claude Simon. His essays on poetry include *Alone with America* (1969), and his 1983 translation of Baudelaire's *Les fleurs du mal* won the American Book Award. He has recently undertaken a new translation of Marcel Proust's *Recherche*.

LAWRENCE D. KRITZMAN, professor of French and the civilization of France at Dartmouth College, is author of *Destruction/
Découverte: Le fonctionnement de la rhétorique dans les "Essais" de
Montaigne* (1980) and editor of two critical anthologies: *Fragments: Incompletion and Discontinuity* (1981) and *Michel Foucault:
Politics, Philosophy, Culture* (1988). He is completing a study on
the intellectual function in France with support from the American Council of Learned Societies.

MARY LYDON, associate professor of French at the University of
Wisconsin, is author of *Perpetuum Mobile: A Study of the Novels
and Aesthetics of Michel Butor* (1980) and editor of *Freud's Imprint*
(*Visible Language* 14/3 [1985]). Her essays have appeared in *Yale
French Studies, Sub-Stance, Humanities in Society,* and *Contempo-
rary Literature.*

BETTY R. MCGRAW is associate professor at Kansas State University, where she teaches French and theory. She has published
numerous articles in *Boundary 2, Sub-Stance, Semiotica,* and the
American Journal of Semiotics. She is coeditor of *RB: Polygraph*
and a coeditor of *Studies in Twentieth Century Literature.* At present, she is working on a revisionist definition of ennui in contemporary French literature.

GARY SHAPIRO, professor of philosophy at the University of Kan-
sas, works in the area of contemporary and nineteenth-century
European philosophy and in the philosophy of literature. He
recently published *Nietzschean Narratives* (Indiana University
Press, 1989). His other essays include "Nietzsche Contra Renan"
(*History and Theory* [1982]), "From the Sublime to the Political"
(*New Literary History* [1985]) and "What Was Literary History?"
(*Social Epistemology* [1988]). He has coedited *Hermeneutics: Ques-
tions and Prospects* (1984) with Alan Sica and is currently editing
a collection of essays on postmodernism.

JEAN-JACQUES THOMAS is professor of literature and Romance
languages at Duke University. He received his Doctorat de 3ᵉ
Cycle in poetics at the Université de Paris. He is editor of "Michel
Leiris," *Sub-Stance,* 11–12 (1975), and author of *Lire Leiris: Essai
d'étude poétique d'un fonctionnement analinguistique* (1972), *Poétique générative* (1978), *La langue la poésie* (1988), and *Yves Bonne-
foy: A New Concordance* (1989). He has also translated Thomas

Sebeok's *Le tissu sémiotique: Chronique des préventions* (1979) and Michael Riffaterre's *Sémiotique de la poésie* (1982) and serves as associate editor of *Sub-Stance* and *Poetics Today.*

STEVEN UNGAR, professor of French and chair of comparative literature at the University of Iowa, is the author of *Roland Barthes: The Professor of Desire* (1983). His writings on French fiction, poetry, and critical theory include articles in *Diacritics, Yale French Studies, Sub-Stance,* and *L'Esprit créateur* as well as the introduction to Jean-Paul Sartre, *"What Is Literature?" and Other Essays* (1988). He is completing book-length projects on Maurice Blanchot and on the cultures of the Popular Front.

SUSAN WARREN is a data communications analyst and artist in Milwaukee.

LORI WOODRUFF, a restaurateur and artist, lives in Milwaukee.

Index

The index refers mainly to names and texts. Other references complement topics and issues engaged in this collection. For primary and secondary bibliographies, see *Communications*, no. 36 (1982); Steven Ungar, *Roland Barthes: The Professor of Desire* (Lincoln: University of Nebraska Press, 1983); and Mary Bittner Wiseman, *The Ecstasies of Roland Barthes* (New York: Routledge, 1989).